SOMETHING TO REMEMBER ME. BYE

More disability frightens me.
Dying I can live with.

Bruce Stasiuk

ACKNOWLEDGMENTS

Cover design and photograph by Donna Crinnian

Edeter Patricia Capon

Rear cover oil portrait by Frederic Thorner

Fly illustrations, paintings, drawings, and Chicken Liver Press logo by me

Chicken Liver Press

NON-DEDICATION

This book has none.
The recipient of my intended dedication warned me.
"Don't."
She celebrates when others are the center of attention.
But not herself.

She's never seeks the spotlight.
Not once have we celebrated her birthday in
a restaurant with a paper crown.
No singing waiters.
No cake. No toasts. No sparklers.
I knew better.

The self-effacing modesty makes me want to dedicate it to her even more.

She's the best person I've ever known.

But I can't.
I won't.
I didn't.

There's no way of knowing the direction my life might have taken had I not stepped onto a trampoline on that Black Friday after Thanksgiving, 1960.

Or

If I hadn't stopped by my sister's house on that Spring day when the girl in the fuzzy pink sweater and tight beige jeans was there.

Would I even be the person I think I am?

Who knows? Not me.

Our lives are full of forks in roads.

Often not aware that one simple turn — a few seconds

—an unlaced shoe, could change everything.

And then there are the forks taken by those who came before us.

Dramatic ones as well as those that appear inconsequential.

If my grandmother had married the stonecutter.

If Diddy wasn't rescued from the cave-in.

If my father hadn't ordered chopped chicken-liver from the cute waitress at that restaurant.

if, if, if…

I wouldn't have written this book, nor would you be reading it.

CONTENTS AND MALCONTENTS

THE STONECUTTER

Anna had a stunning face and a dancer's body. She knew. It was confirmed in the repeated glances and hopeful politeness of men. It made her confident and daring.

It made her mother protective. Marie interrupted the glances before they became stares.

Wearing a summer dress, Anna walked past the brick wall of the Piccirilli foundry on 142nd Street. The six stonecutters had come to the South Bronx in 1887, brought by their father, Giuseppe.

The two heavy gates, parting like open arms sweeping over the sidewalk, pushed her pathway closer to the curb. The light cotton fabric contouring with each step.

Anna listened to the silent compliment of resting chisels as she walked past the steel curtains and their concrete stage.

The gates found reason to be open each afternoon during her strolls to Saint Mary's Park, and the mallets paused as she went by.

The audience of brothers let their interests be known.

Bellissimo!

Bello!

Dolce!

Good shapes were in their blood.

Anna would smile at their strange words, then continue onto the park. Upon reaching Brook Avenue, she'd hear the distant clatter of tools starting up again.

One of the brothers finally engaged Anna's attention.

It started with a simple escort to the edge of the park where they sat for lunch.

Soon, they were spending early evenings walking under the trees.

They found a catch of neglected grass, surrounded by huge, half-buried boulders.

It became their place.

One night they sat there through a thin rain, while she told of her dancing.

He explained that the elephant-sized stones sheltering them were *quarzo* and *feldspato*. He promised to cut "Anna" into the largest one.

Those moments together brought them to a deep romance.

They shared enough language to talk of marriage, asking for Marie's blessing.

He was a good, hardworking man.

Marie approved.

But the passionate relationship could not survive Anna's rash independence. After a simple misunderstanding flared into a cold argument, she exercised her spite by running off with Pete Ricarrdi, a much older gentleman who had been pursuing her for some time.

Pete wore woolen suits, unlike the dusty apron of the stonecutter.

He so enjoyed the pleasure of having a lovely young bride, he quickly expressed his excitement by making her pregnant.

The war ended and new customers were marching home, toting duffel bags over their shoulders, and the Spanish flu in their lungs.

The radio called it "The Influenza." It killed millions, including Anna, on the very day her child, Josephine, was born.

Pete, wanting a young woman, not a young burden, went off for fresh adventures.

Josephine was taken in by her grandmother, Marie, Anna's grieving mother. She was raised in the stern, but secure, Alsatian way. Dancing lessons were arranged.

Entering her teens, Josephine's curiosity about her real mother grew as Marie's memory was wearing down from age, and the brutal fall down the stone stairs of Beech Terrace.

Marie could recall the furious love affair with the tombstone cutter, but she lost his first name to time. It was just Mr. Piccirilli. She remembered how he wept into his hat.

By the time the story was told to me, pieces had been chipped away.

My mother, Josephine, explained that the foundry was where it all began… and ended.

It was where I played stickball.

The rusty hinge was the third base foul line. Our game would pause whenever the gates reluctantly wobbled to an open clank, followed by a truck growling its way through.

The carvers still worked there, but people said a few of them had died.

The others were getting old.

The hammers finally stopped before we moved away.

We shared our Sunday breakfast of eggs, toast, and newspapers.

After turning the page from, *The Millennium Bug, the Y2K Menace,* I saw the photo.

The foundry. The caption confirmed it, except "studio" was the word used.

"Look at this picture! In the paper! The Bronx. It's where I used to play stickball on 142nd street.

It's where the stonecutters worked. My grandmother was engaged to one of them."

My wife put her paper down.

We read the article.

"The colossal figure of Abraham Lincoln that broods in Washington's Lincoln Memorial was carved at what is now a vacant lot in the Bronx, one of the works of the Italian-born Piccirilli brothers…Attilio, Furio, Orazio, Ferrucio, Getulio, and Masaniello… who left their mark as sculptors all over America…"

The Piccirilli brothers.
One of them
never became my grandfather.

Some other works done by the brothers at the 142 St. studio.

Washington Square Arch

Tomb of the Unknown Soldier

My mother took dancing lessons.

THREE SIXTY-TWO

Josephine was born an orphan. It was 1918, the year of the Great Pandemic. Within hours of her birth, the flu killed her mother, and her father, Pete, disappeared.

Marie buried her daughter and took her grandchild in. She raised Josephine along with her own teenage children, Claire and Charlie.

Marie owned 362 Willis Avenue in the South Bronx. The building housed her grocery and dry goods store. Burlap sacks filled with grains, beans, and spices lined the wooden floor beside barrels of pickles, olives, and ceramic tubs of sauerkraut. Above the shop was a storage area, with apartments on the third and fourth floors.

Years later, while bringing soup to Josephine, who was now married and a mother herself, Marie stumbled on the stone steps leading up to Beech Terrace, and by protecting the soup, failed to protect herself.
She became what was called, an 'invalid.'

The business closed down. Brown paper covered the windows. It sat for years. After being discharged from the army, Charlie reopened it as the Willis Radio Store.
He sold appliances along with the radios.
Josephine moved into the third-floor apartment with her husband, daughter, and me, her son.
Although I wasn't born there, my memories were.
It was where I first saw my father's face while he was on military furlough.
During my early years, it was the place where my mother would bathe me in the kitchen sink because our bathroom was off the hallway.

The door to the building, which opened onto the sidewalk, was never locked, nor was the door to our apartment.

We had a living room, a kitchen, and two bedrooms. The smaller bedroom occasionally housed Marie when Claire was exhausted from tending to her. My grandmother needed lots of care. She was hard to understand because her words were caught between an Alsatian accent and the head injury.

My mother distributed linens stamped with *Consolidated Laundries* to the mystery people who lived upstairs. They were there, then they'd be gone, replaced by other mystery people. My mother called them tenants.

Olga was one. A heavy woman who wore black. I'd try to beat her to the front door. Walking up the two flights behind Olga's slow waddle took forever for a kid who usually did three steps at a time. It was worse if she stopped at the ledge where the mail was left unsorted. I couldn't fit around her.

Those stairs brought the seltzer man.

I could hear him outside our door with the brittle clinking of his blue bottles. I knew it wasn't the milkman because my father was the milkman. He delivered for Chesterfield Farms.

Once, while in his white uniform, a crowd, thinking he was a doctor, pushed him to the front after two cars collided near the corner.

The real doctor was Doctor Green. When I was sick, I went to him. When I was very sick, he came to me, toting his black leather bag of cures. I always got better.

Mr. Picininni would pull up in his square truck, flip a burlap rag over his shoulder, and claw his tongs into a massive block of ice, crystal splinters flying off. He'd swing it onto his shoulder and lug it up to a tenant's icebox. He never stopped at our door.

We had a refrigerator.

The war ended, and Uncle Charlie was doing very well.

He started selling more televisions and fewer radios. In a few years, we'd have our own TV. It was a heavy piece of wooden furniture with a screen the size of a piece of toast. The three channels lit up for several hours each day.

Part of growing up was suddenly noticing things that were always there. The dainty pipe stumps coming out of the walls were like that. One evening my father took a match from the tin container above the stove, and while turning the valve, lit one of the pipes. The gaslights still worked.

In the evenings we'd compete for the big leather chair stationed at our front window overlooking the straight avenue. Willis was a true Avenue. A wide thoroughfare with a cobblestone street laid by the Dutch. A pair of unused trolley tracks were set in the stone. I loved the sound of tires as they riveted their way past our stage. I studied each bus as it stopped on the corner.
The doors would hiss open and I'd hope that this would be the one my mother would step from after selling candy to the wealthy Grand Concourse folks at Barton's Bonbonire.

Coal trucks backed up onto the sidewalk. The quickly assembled chutes used gravity and a man's shovel to deliver rumbling coal to the open bulkhead doors. Pedestrians stood there, waiting, fumbling with cigarettes, rather than walking around the trucks and onto the busy avenue.
A heavy wagon pulled by a horse slowed the traffic. Hooves clopping against the polished stones while dropping 'street apples' for the tough kids to throw. During cold days, the manure would give off wisps of steam.

The cardboard man came with his pushcart to collect boxes from the appliances Uncle Charlie sold.
One cold afternoon, he came with a woman. She laid down in the wagon and he covered her with piles of bent and folded cardboard to keep her warm as she slept.
I watched it all from the big chair. I was confused by its sadness and beauty.

The tavern on the corner provided scary theater on some evenings. During the day, a door might open, leaking dark stale belches of cool.

Across the way, next to the army and navy store, was the smoke shop with the big cigar sign.

My father sent me there to buy two Optimos whenever Aunt Bertha and Uncle Joe came to visit in their black 1920 Buick. It had flower vases and portable screens to keep bugs out when they went to the drive-in.

People slowed their pace whenever it was parked on Willis.

My father sent me on missions to the *Chinese*. It was an apartment two blocks away. I'd walk up four flights, knock on the door, hand the man my father's envelope, then sit on the wobbly chair in the hallway and wait. The door would eventually open and the man would hand me a warm bag. I'd scurry home with dinner.

Sometimes I was sent to the grocery store with a note for two quarts of *Ballantine Beer*. The grocer would complain, but always sell it to me. The brown paper bag had the price written in black crayon on the side. I was embarrassed every time I went on that errand.

The Tip Top pole spun when the shop was open. From the booster seat, I wondered why the barbers had so little hair. The funnel-like spittoons were placed right under the infinity of mirrors which amazed me. I'd try to move swiftly enough to look deeper into the reflections...always failing. After every haircut, the barber would show me a piece of my ear that he accidentally cut off. It never hurt and I never bled.

But mostly I remember the evenings when I had the heavy leather chair to myself.

I'd look out at the night and across the street to those big windows and the colorless room. It was always — almost always — empty and quiet. No one was there.

But sometimes, just sometimes, on the school-less weekends, I'd stay up late and it would glisten and glow. Music poured from the opened windows. I could hear shouts, laughter, and cheers mixed in with the clattering of dishes and glasses.

One loud voice would boom into the silence, followed by clapping and more laughter. The crowd moved to the speed of music. Some people would spill out onto the sidewalk. Men wore ties and women were in crayon colors. They would touch and yell. They'd cry and punch and kiss. I could see the pumpkin glow from their cigarettes. I'd leave the viewing stand and go to bed, resting on the magical sounds which carried me into sleep.

In the morning it was all gone. The music, the people, the sounds. It was silent once again, and the closed windows were dull and empty.

Charlie, Claire, Marie, Josephine

Marie in her store.

1948

My steps were much shorter than his.

It was hard keeping up.

Even more difficult in the August heat.

Still, my father wore a hat.

All men did.

The tall, grey, concrete wall turned gently to my left and went on forever.

It was a long walk.

There were no windows to look in.

No reflections off glass.

People from behind, walking faster, passed us on the sidewalk.

They quickly disappeared around the curve.

I could hear soft voices, not knowing where they came from.

Then, there it was.

The crowd. Waiting.

Standing in line outside the large open passageway.

We joined. We were last, but not for long.

Soon there were more people standing behind us, and fewer in front.

I had no problem keeping the pace now, with slow, short, rocking steps as we entered through the big doorway.

The sounds were whispers. Soft coughs. Shoes scratching along the concrete floor.

I could smell the flowers before seeing them.

Policemen wearing white gloves were standing still.

Tall candles rose from a jungle of green feathery leaves.

People in front of us, stopped, stood, stared down, then walked away from the long, shiny box.

My father looked into it.

I couldn't.

He heaved me up onto his forearm.

The man was sleeping.

Not moving.

When we got back to our car, my father stopped, turned to me, and said,

"He hit more home runs than anyone."

THE APOLOGY

It rained that day. The game at Ebbets Field was called before the first inning, so I never got to see the Dodgers play.
Brooklyn was far from the Bronx and my father loved his Yankees.
Baseball meant getting 'sick,' skipping school, and going to the Stadium.
My father always wore his hat and I always carried my catcher's mitt.
The field was full of stunning colors I never saw on Willis Avenue.

Deep into each game my father would listen for the 'pop' of the bullpen pitchers warming up, or the starters going through their off-day routine. We'd take the long walk to the concrete pit where we could watch the battery boys up close.
It was there I saw Bob Feller.
He was high kicking as his pitches sizzled past us, creating a puff of dust from the catcher's mitt.
Then it happened.
My father asked me to say things.
I didn't want to, but he urged me on.
I wasn't happy, but I obediently did it.
He'd put words into my ear and I was to yell them.
I didn't know what I was shouting, but I knew the things were not good by the look on Bob Feller's face.

"Hey, what happened with the White Sox?"

A few of the other players were smirking.
My father fed me more lines.

"Hey Bob, what about those two World Series games you lost?"

"Hey Bob, are you losing it?"

He stopped pitching and slowly walked over to me.

I was scared.

He looked up and asked, "Hey kid, did you come to see the game?"

Nervously, I answered, "Yes."

He growled, "Then go watch it!"

Frightened, I leaned back, and the mitt slipped from my hand, falling into the pit where I'd never see it again.

The catcher walked over and picked it up. I was sure he was going to present it to Bob Feller as a trophy.

Instead, he tossed the mitt up to me.

Jolted, but relieved, we went back to watching the game.

The newspaper article said he was healthy at 91, spending much of his time at the Bob Feller Baseball Museum in Van Meter Iowa.

He was still alive, and I had an address. The Museum.

My father was long gone, but my discomfort resurfaced. Telling no one of the apology, I mailed it, hoping it would get into his hands. Even if it didn't, I felt better.

Months later, while watching a Yankee game, the phone rang.

"Hello. Can I speak to Bruce Stasiuk?"

"I'm Bruce."

"This is Bob Feller.

"Bob Feller?"

"Yes. I received your letter recently. Thanks. That was very nice of you."

"I can't believe that you actually called."

"Well, it was a special letter."

After chatting, I said, "Next time you're in New York I'd love to have you come over for dinner."

"That's kind of you, but I can't do much travelling anymore. But if you come out this way, I'll give you a personal tour of my museum."

I didn't mention that travel was becoming difficult for me too.

"Well, I just want you to know that I accept your apology. You can now relax."

He laughed.

"Gee, I'm so sorry. I was just a kid. I didn't even know what my father was telling me to say."

"Hey, like I said, I accept your apology."

He laughed, then added, "Oh…and I'm glad you got your catcher's mitt back."

With my first catcher's mitt.

UNCLE JACK

"We have a dead Caucasian male. Apparent bullet wound to the chest."

He was found behind the steering wheel, head angled back, a jelly donut anchored between his teeth.

No. It wasn't blood.

He wasn't shot.

It was a heart attack.

The "bullet-hole" was a dried clot of raspberry filling that dripped onto his shirt. His vehicle was a hearse, and the contents indicated that it was his home too.

Early on I realized there was something different about Uncle Jack.

He had a soft, pale, sandbag body.

The tip of his nose looked like an inverted valentine, resembling a little pair of buttocks, crack and all. It was both hideous and amazing. My eyes always fixed on it. Maybe that explains why he never looked at me much beyond a glance. Except for the nose, he was ordinary looking. Nondescript. Average height and weight. But there was nothing else average about him.

He spoke fast, compressing conversations, rarely offering the courtesy of a comma.

As he flooded the air with words, his eyes scanned the room like an oscillating fan, hunting for a larger audience. Uncle Jack was always trolling to see who wasn't listening. Since the adults weren't, he aimed for us, his nieces and nephews; little pairs of ears to be filled.

Some said he was crazy. Not wrist-restraint crazy… but odd.

Did he really beat his oldest daughter with an ax handle for misbehaving?

Was his constant ridicule the cause of his youngest son's uncontrollable stutter?

He was the relative the aunts and uncles whispered about.

Those whispers eventually blossomed into open comments. They were insults really, which he seemed to accept as endorsements.

We turned off the Garden State Parkway at Kenilworth, following the map to 14 Odessa. My mother was certain that we were at the right place. She looked back at the note.

"14 Odessa Street. It says it right here."

But this was a junkyard, filled with car hulks, rust-glazed cast iron pipes, pieces of washing machines, rolls of tar paper, clusters of cinder blocks, and organs from retired appliances. Along the rutted dirt driveway were pieces of upholstered furniture soaking up the rain like bread in gravy.
My father cautiously nosed the Buick around the bigger holes, hoping that some scar-faced dog wouldn't chew the tires off our car. There was no dog, just a shirtless Uncle Jack.
He waved at us with his wrench.

He explained that he was making final adjustments on the abandoned bicycle-propelled, stainless steel chest he recently salvaged. The type an ice cream vendor would pedal around a park. He converted the insulated chest into a one-wheeled sidecar for his motorcycle.

"It has to be tested immediately."

While pulling the goggles down from his forehead, he pointed to me and said,

"You're the right size. Get in."

We took a trial run, spluttering down the muddy driveway and out into the street, followed by belching black smoke.

So, this was the country home we'd heard about.

The wooden shingles were returning back to nature, and the roof would soon be covered with soil because Uncle Jack thought it to be a perfect place to grow grass. He experimented with the idea, which partly explained the tobacco-colored stains on the ceilings.

Before dinner, Uncle Jack instructed how to squat, and get up without using arms, like he did on the Indian reservation.
He explained how he had been taking pictures of Niagara Falls after climbing the tour boat's mast. The security guards pulled him down and escorted him off.

I moved the food about on the plate but not into my mouth.
Everything about the place warned me not to eat.
As badly as I needed to use the toilet, I wouldn't. The murky toilet water rose and fell, pulsing, breath-like, to the rhythm of some force. The seatless bowl had several high-water marks. The flush-bucket contained water borrowed from the neighbors, since the well no longer pumped. I clamped up, hoping for an early departure tomorrow.

I slept with my four cousins on a floor mat.
In the morning, I was awakened to soiled underwear and laughter. It was kinder to be teased than to state the truth; I refused to use the stained, dark, dripping bathroom.
After avoiding breakfast, I was glad to be leaving.

Uncle Jack approached me beside the car.

"Open your hand."

I reluctantly obeyed.
He placed a flat, shiny square — about the size of a baby's fingernail — in my hand.

"Look at the future."

I looked.

"It's called a chip…a silicon chip. It will change the World."

I was not impressed.

Our car slalomed its way around the puddled ruts as we waved goodbye.
I never saw him again.

I heard Uncle Jack took his last Thanksgiving dinner outside, naked in one
of his car shells, while his family sat at the table. He said he wanted to dine
with God.

Last I heard, my aunt divorced him and the kids left.
Escaped maybe.

Uncle Jack

CONSANGUINITY

That's the word.

Yeah. Consanguinity.

I used it.

Done, lacking the confidence to even properly pronounce it or grasp its meaning.

It was in the dictionary and was impressive.

If I used it, maybe I'd be impressive too.

Families talk about the first one who ever went to college.

I was the family's first high school graduate.

My mother called me a genius.

I wasn't.

She was comparing me to my sister.

I didn't know what to call what I was writing, but it held tight to the margin, sitting on the page like a poem.

I added 'that' word and submitted it to the literary magazine, along with a few other things,

They liked it enough to invite me to their next meeting.

It was held in the upstairs apartment of a house near the college.

The editor met me at the door, introducing himself as Mister Manheim.

Mister…even though he appeared to be about 20. My age.

There were enough people to fill the small room, the chairs, and the carpet.

I was a fraud, mixing with the school's literary elite.

One guy wore thick glasses which made his eyes looked raisin small. He smoked a pipe.

They chatted over white wine and cheese cubes before the readings started.

Some were about death. Some about eternity. Some claimed that warfare was not good.

Some were about something.

The girl with the scarf read her poem. It included the word 'verdant'.

The brown-overalls girl said,

"Oh God…I adore that word…verdant. It paints such a lush, green picture."

HHeads nodded in agreement.
We all read. Me too.
But not the one with my special word.
The last presentation was the magazine's editor, Mr. Manheim.
Everyone was attentive as he read his piece, 'Clouds'.
I remember one line.

"The butter sun melts into the muffin clouds, then gently floats away."

Leaving, I still felt like a fraud.
I was in good company.

DIDDY

The Ukrainian word for grandfather was difficult for the kids to pronounce.
It came out, 'Diddy'.

Sitting at the end of the table, he'd eat kasha, yogurt, and sliced apples; a diet
the doctor prescribed for the small hole in his heart.
We had kielbasa, holubtsi, and Bobcha's pirogues.
A bowl of beet-reddened horseradish was always within reach.
After dinner, he'd sleep, even while sunlight sliced through the Venetian blinds.
Bobcha said we children were to be quiet.

Diddy came from the Ukraine. It was called *The Ukraine* back then, as if it
were the possession of others.
History says it was.

He left around 1904, not yet centered into his teens.
After packing, he gave the family a final embrace.
Looking at his mother, he said, "Goodbye."
Both knew it meant forever.
He closed the door to his home, its dirt floor, embroidered cloth, and rustic tools.

Taking a wagon to a town, then another wagon to a larger town, he worked
his way to a place bold enough to have tracks.
The train traveled to Bremen, a teeming port where the namesake ship was
steadied by its harness. He had never seen anything like this in Torske.
Not even in the big city, Ternopil.
This place was so full for the senses.
The Bremen leaned against the very ocean which would deliver him to the
land of promise.
He paid the boarding fee to a bearded man who was wearing finger-less
gloves and a dark coat.

Documents were stamped and re-stamped before securing them deeply into his pocket.

The dock groaned to the water's rhythm as passengers were herded aboard. The ship squeaked impatiently, rubbing against the pilings. A departure horn rattled his chest.

This mighty vessel would take him but one way, outpacing the steam pouring from its funnel. The frothy cut in the water parted like a gusty wheat field. He looked back toward his world, family, friends, language, until the city was lost in vapor.

He was welcomed into the coal mines of central Pennsylvania, where words were not needed.

Muscle was … brute, hungry muscle.

Quickly advancing from culler to miner, he rode the trolly deep into the shaft each day. The humming ventilator fed the mine with breathable air, while the engine pumped encroaching water out.

After taking his first few strikes at the abutment, the support timbers exploded —splintered — and the earth folded in. A chorus of shrieks and fading groans were buried in black silence.

He felt the stings and warm drip on his forehead. He blotted his fingers against his face looking for blood. He couldn't see his hand, inches from his eyes. Was he blind?

The dark was unlike any before. He called out.

His arms and legs searched for space — finding little.

He screamed.

He had nothing. Nothing but thought. For hours. Sleeping. Opening eyes to nothing. He ached for his home, his village. He imagined his mother's piercing sadness when told of her little boy and how his dreams were crushed and drowned in an airless grave. He held on in the lightless pocket, moving little and searching for the next thin gulp of life. One more breath of fading air. Then another.

The thirst and hunger grew, suggesting it was days.
He was too young to die now.

And then, something.

The soft pattern came from above. It grew louder. Then strange voices. The ping of hammers against rock.
Hollow tubes pounded and pushed through the shale, hoping to deliver breath.
Then, a break-through with a trace of sweet light.

Between the approaching thuds he could hear his insides begging for water, just a sip from an unreachable puddle that was feet away.

He never went into the mine again.

Farming. Barbering. Finally, the diner.

I sat in the black Chrysler with its big woolen seats and watched him move the round wooden handle of the gearshift as his feet worked the pedals.
We drove away from 'Steve's Diner' where the floor was covered with sawdust and the cellar stored barrels of fermenting cabbage.
We went up the hill.
Beneath his healed wounds blue strokes were tattooed into his flesh from the powdery chunks of falling anthracite.
I wanted marks on my face too.
His low and tilted eyelids gave him the look of an Eskimo.
Torske was always there in the shape of his words.
The coal dust never left his soft voice.

When he laughed, I could see gold flashing in his mouth.
We turned onto the Grand Concourse and Harry the cop waved.
Diddy was important.

Thinking of Bobcha's words, "If you want to see him alive…" I drove north-bound through thickening snow.

Even with huge plows working into evening, the turnpike challenged all the way to Albany.

I could hear the groan before entering the room.

He was staring at the ceiling.

I followed a tube that crossed his chest and was tangled in his hands.

Were they always this big? Thick, and meaty like a bear's.

When his head flopped to the right, our eyes met.

He spoke to me in the language I never learned.

Bobcha made the journey with his ashes and cast them into the Ukrainian wind.

The Bremen brought him to America.

Some of the family he left in Ukraine.

Diddy never went down into the mine again.
He leans against the window of his barber shop.

Me by Diddy's car.

His diner was near Yankee Stadium.

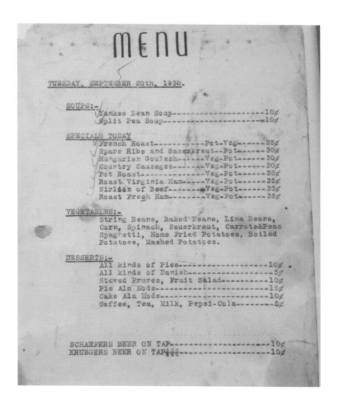

A dollar went a long way.

ONE SECOND

My body could do almost anything. I knew it early on.

Stickball was a big sport on 142nd Street.

When sides were chosen, I'd never be picked first.

Playing with the much older guys put me in my place, but only for a while.

When my father drove me to tryouts for the Yankee Stadium Little League, I had to lie my way into the strange and fancy uptown neighborhood by using Diddy's address. The coaches gathered the players for tryouts.

As I started throwing and hitting, a crowd formed.

The coaches drew numbers from a lottery, and Manny, a round, balding businessman, won the first pick. He selected me. My father let people know I was his son.

My team was sponsored by Terri-Lee, a woman's clothing company. I was one of three kids who were invited to an elegant office building for a promotional photo. The other two boys showed up wearing suits. I wore my street clothes. One executive invited me to take off my coat. I declined. Sensing my embarrassment, he suggested that I probably wanted to keep my throwing-arm warm.

I was ashamed to let them see that I was wearing a tee shirt underneath.

My parents let me down. The picture appeared in *The Daily News*.

I wasn't smiling.

The season went well. Our field was in the Stadium's shadow. The Yankees would occasionally come to watch our games.

Their catcher, Elston Howard, will yell out encouragement to me, a member of his masked fraternity.

Sometimes the guys back on 142nd would play ball on the dirt field at Randall's Island.

After one sweaty game, they cooled off in the East River. I didn't.

"Wassamatter, you can't swim?"

"I can swim."

"Then com'on in."

Truth was that I didn't know how, and this wouldn't be a perfect place to learn, with its fickle currents and floating prophylactics, known to us as 'East River Whitefish.'

Later that month, I undressed to the hypnotic smell of pool water. After putting my clothes in a wire basket, the attendant handed me an elastic ankle-band supporting a numbered brass medallion. I followed the hurried jangles of others, first, into the showers to wash off the Bronx, then, after many turns and corners, into the large hangar which domed the pool.

Coming from a world of grey concrete and a colorless river, the pool glowed. That glimmering blue stunned me, much like the green jolt of grass on my first view of Yankee Stadium. The air had the trustworthy bite of chlorine.

Smitty, the head lifeguard, wore an orange, woolen bathing suit. It hung, supported by shoulder straps, over his large black body. A blue stripe went from his armpit to his thigh. When he blew his whistle, most noise and motion stopped. Quiet, shivering kids would stand outside the pool until he'd finish his slow, walk-around-the-pool lecture about the fine art of water etiquette. But some kids never left the pool.

They were members of the Porpoise Club, the Saint Mary's Park swim team. I learned to swim that day. Within two weeks I was a member of the Porpoise Club.

After one winter practice session, I watched a diving instructor struggling with an awkward student. The rumor was that Frank was an NYU coach who had trained a diver named Freddie Munch for the Olympic trials. He was not having much success this night.

After noticing me, off to the side, pacing my way through his instructions, he invited me into his lesson. I never saw the other student again, but I saw Frank a lot. Four nights a week for the next two years.

I came to smell like chlorine, and my hair became straw colored.

I hardly ever got to 142nd anymore.

For those two years it was,

"Approach. Right knee higher. Elevate. Tighter tuck. Straighter knees. Point the toes.

Let the board work for you. Cut the water. "

I'd air-dry as Frank would diagnose each dive.

"You have to keep the feet together. Reduce the splash. Too much motion in the ocean! Elevate. Tighter. Better form. Closer to the board."

Although I learned diving during those two years, the lonely, wet lessons owned me.

The pool entertained hundreds during the day, but it was mine alone each night.

Just coach and me. His words echoing off the tiled walls.

I rarely went straight home after school. I'd take the lonely walk from Saint Pius School to the Park for another evening with Frank and the one-meter board.

I'd pass brick factories on one side, and a hospital, set far back from the street, on the other. I never knew what was going on behind the high, tobacco-colored factory windows, but I was told that the men in pajamas sitting on the elevated balconies of the hospital had a coughing disease called Tuberculosis. TB for short.

I'd put on my diving suit in the empty locker room.

Frank would be waiting by the pool.

We'd practice the routine dives and work on the newest.

"More elevation. Tighter tuck. Let the board do the work."

During one session, I hit the board while doing a cutaway. Still loaded with my momentum, it snapped back striking my forehead.
I walked home, passing the brick factory walls in the winter darkness. I looked at the hospital balconies, which were always empty after practice.
I'd wonder if the men had died while I was diving.
I kept thinking until I reached home.
The next night I didn't show up.
Or the next.
Or the next.
I never went back to the pool.

The following month, Saint Mary's installed a trampoline in the main building.
I went with some friends to see the marvel.
As I was bouncing on it, Frank walked in.

"Sometimes you have to face the music."

That was all he said. I looked at the floor until he was gone. The shame hurt.
It was the last time I ever saw him.

Back to 142nd for me. Until we moved out of the Bronx.
My family may have been a part of what urban history later called, 'White Flight.' Ronkonkoma was the Promised Land.
This place had a lake with diving boards and girls.
I made friends. Joe, Alphy. Johnny.
We played games and hung out at the lake
My body was changing.
I won the bet with Joe, when I raised the front end of his mother's Renault sedan off the ground.

Alphy and Johnny knew things that I didn't, like the Sun being closer to Earth in the winter.

But I could lift their whole set of weights over my head with one arm.

At fourteen, muscle trumped brains.

Pete, the lifeguard, once asked me to take over the beach. It was a cloudy day with few swimmers, and he wanted to do things to a girl in the locker room.

Wearing my fast-drying diving suit, I sat up on the lifeguard stand.

Pete had seen me dive in the swim meets held at the lake each year.

After thanking me, he explained a new dive.

A 'Flying A.'

It was one I never did with Frank.

The classroom was dull, but the gym wasn't. I made the basketball team.

I felt the cartilage in my knee tearing during one game, but I didn't tell Coach Hazen.

I played linebacker on the football team and went to the coach's summer camp in Maine.

One night we went to the Bangor Fair. A barker sold tickets to see the exotic woman in the tent. Those who paid an extra dollar could stay to see her smoke a cigarette in an unusual way. I saw the show twice. I was sixteen.

We ran through drills every day.

After practice, Coach Schnell called me into his office to tell me that I was the most coordinated athlete he had ever seen.

"Bruce, you're gonna' go places."

Dancing at weddings was easy. It was just another sport.

My mother would brag about her son to the butchers she worked with.

They were used to carting sides of beef from the truck.

At their annual Christmas party, they decided to silence her. They each challenged me to an arm-wrestling match.

I beat them all.

During the summer, I played baseball at Newton Field.
I was catcher on the Suffolk County All-Star team.
Frank Staub saw me play.
Frank, who was the manager of the Ronkonkoma Cardinals, —– a semi-pro team with two Yastrzemskis playing the infield —– asked my father if I could catch for his team next year, when I'd turn seventeen. Frank was going to retire, and the Cardinals needed a catcher.
I was set.

Alphy and Johnny had met Larry while I was away at football camp. When the summer ended, the brothers went back to Queens, leaving Larry for me. On the Friday after Thanksgiving, he called.

"Hey, you wanna' go to a movie with me and Maryann?"

Maryann was his sexy and slightly overweight cousin. She was years older than us and was engaged to some guy in the City. She used to flirt with me when I was up on the lifeguard stand. Once, a bunch of us were in a car together. Maryann was sitting next to me in the back seat. She took off her jacket and tented it over our heads.
She passionately kissed me while moaning. This confirmed what Larry told me.

"Sure. What time can you pick me up?"

On the way to the Commack Movie Theater, we saw a trampoline center.
I talked Larry into stopping.
The attendant asked, "Have you ever used a trampoline?"

"Once."

Maryann sat on a bench. Larry bobbled and fell a few times. My first attempt was awkward. I tried again. I used my years of diving…my nights with Frank…

"*Get altitude…more height…tight toes…straight knees…watch form.*"

I did Pete's 'Flying A'.
"*Arms far out to side. Slight bend at waist. Rotate. Point toes. Shoulders in.*"

It took a second.
There was no water.

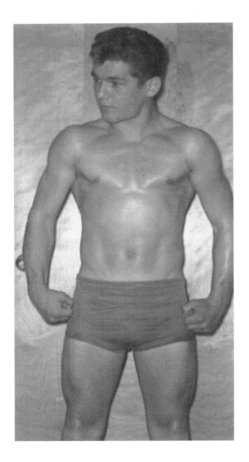

In my diving suit at fifteen

Yankee Stadium little league tryout day. Me with hat pushed back.

Three New York Yankees and the Bronx D.A.

Two Carl Yastrzemskis Swinging for Cardinals

FATHER & SON have been playing regularly for the Lake Ronkonkoma Cardinals during their Suffolk County Baseball league schedule this season. They are Carl, Jr., left, and Carl, Sr., Yastrzemski of Bridgehampton. Both men are batting well over .400 in league play. They handle the shortstop and third-base duties, respectively.

I was going to be the catcher for the Ronkonkoma Cardinals.

Promotional photo for the New York Yankees Little League.

The only time I made the front page.

THE WOMAN

It happened soon after my accident.

I was prone on the Stryker Frame which had two positions, facing the ceiling or the floor.

The nurses rotated me every few hours… like a chicken on a barbecue spit… to prevent, or minimize…the development of bed sores.

I was paralyzed below the neck, right down to my soles.

No motion.

No sensation.

My face, surrounded and anchored by the fabric donut, couldn't take in much beyond the linoleum tiles.

First, I heard the unmistakably feminine clack of heels. Not a common hospital room sound.

Then, I could see the legs.

Beautiful legs.

The mirror was positioned on the floor, under me, and angled upright, like a book propped up on a lectern.

It was there to help me see who I was talking to. But only if the nurse, doctor, or visitor would stand in the right place.

This wasn't a nurse.

My eyes went from black high heels, to long calves, to a wool skirt that stopped at the knees. I didn't stop at the knees. I went as high as the reflected light carried, then let my imagination take over.

She explained that her father, who had a heart attack, was also a patient in the hospital.

There was talk about the young athlete's accident and she wanted to meet me.

"Do you mind if I sit with you for a while?"

"No. I don't mind."

She positioned the chair near me.

I could now see up to her shoulders as she told me about herself.

Her fiancée was an entertainer in the army, somewhere. I think she mentioned Africa.

In a year or so, he'd be discharged, and they'd plan the wedding.

She shifted the chair forward so that eye contact was made.

Pretty face.

Thin, straight nose.

Blue eyes.

Brown, disciplined hair.

I thought of the Breck Shampoo models in the magazine ads.

Maybe 25.

I was a 17-year-old kid.

Before leaving, she asked, "Would you mind if I stopped by again?"

"Nope. I'll be here."

We both laughed.

Face down, I recognized the sound of the approaching heels the next day.

She knew where to stand so I could see her.

Soon the chair was positioned as we talked.

Being face up during the third visit, I took in the full picture.

Well dressed…like a woman.

Trim.

Beautiful face and expressions.

Nice, straight teeth.

Long white fingers.

Elegant.

Perfect.

Not like the high school girls I knew.

She fed me some chocolates.

She came the next day.
And the next.

She stopped asking if she could visit.
She just did.
The visits continued long after her father's discharge.
Sometimes during the day, while my parents were working, and most every evening.

She told me more about Richard, her fiancée. How they met. Their plans.
She asked me about my high school, the teams, the girls, the accident.
She had much more to say than I did, and she said it better.
Our conversations reminded me just how immature I was.
She never mentioned it.

When the pelvic fragments were harvested from my hip, wired between my damaged cervical vertebrae, and finally fused and stabilized, it was time to end my two-month stay at the general hospital and be transported to Haverstraw.

The rehabilitation hospital was eighty miles from my home.
As high school classmates were surely loading up station wagons and being driven off to college, my cardboard box of possessions was placed in the ambulance under my stretcher.
I was nervous.
My mother sat by my side.
Only years later, did I realize how sad this trip was for her.

The woman made the trips with my parents, almost every week.
Sometimes she drove alone.
One hundred and sixty miles…round trip.

The guys in the ward might have thought she was my girlfriend, even though our ages didn't make sense. Maybe they figured that she was just a very affectionate sister.

Either way, they didn't stop staring.

Red, the nasty orderly, let out wolf sounds every time she came.

After six months, the hospital decided to release me on weekends.

Their thinking was that it was wise to start making adjustments to life at home…the real world.

I regained some movement and sensation.

I could feed myself.

She shared the driving with my parents.

Now it was two weekly round trips.

Picking me up every Friday and returning me every Sunday night.

Sometimes she did it alone.

She often slept at our house.

This routine went on for more than a year.

I knew he'd be coming home within days.

Things would surely change.

She had to get on with her life.

I was laying in the high hospital bed that a community agency loaned my parents. It couldn't fit into my bedroom, so I slept in the knotty-pine den during my weekend stays.

It was late.

Everyone was asleep.

She entered the room wearing a bathrobe, stood by the side of my raised bed, and looked at me.

She worked her hip up, onto the mattress and rubbed my arm as she pressed against me.

She stroked my face with the back of her hand.

Bending over, she put her cheek against mine and slowly moved it back and forth.

She started kissing my face.

Slow, gentle, little kisses.

I started kissing her neck.

We said nothing.

She leaned into me, breathing heavily.

I said, "C'mon."

"C'mon what?"
"You know."

"I'm not sure. What if I do the wrong thing?"

"It won't be. You won't."

"How can I be sure?"

"C'mon. You know."

She untied her bathrobe.

I looked at the smooth skin of her breasts and her naked body.

The bathrobe was still hanging from her shoulders.

As she rolled them back, one by one, it fully opened and fell to the bed.

We kissed as she got on top of me.

Months of passion poured out.

Afterwards, she sat up, walked over to the upholstered chair on the other side of my bed, took out a cigarette, and lit it.

Watching me stare at her body, she took deep and slow draws on her cigarette,
letting the smoke drift up toward the ceiling.
We said nothing.
She sat like that until the cigarette was finished.

It was finished.

He came home and she was gone.
They got married.

If she's alive…she'd be in her 80's.
I think of her sometimes.

A PARABLE, SPOILED

Bob was my closest friend in high school.
He lived in one of Sayville's stately homes.
I rode the bus from Ronkonkoma.

His father was a commander in the navy.
Mine drove a propane truck.

We both played varsity basketball and football.
He was the captain on both teams.

After graduating, he attended Annapolis, becoming an officer.
I was in a rehabilitation hospital relearning to feed myself.

Bob had deep faith in God.
I had none.
He believed The Creator made man.
I saw it the other way around.

He'd visit, trying to salvage my soul.
I wanted to reward his efforts, but I just couldn't.
His caring attempts stirred up new objections from me.
I was not to be saved.

But he didn't give up.
During one visit, he told a parable about two men and a priest.

One asked, "Father, can I smoke while praying?"
The priest frowned, "No. That would be sacrilegious."
The other asked, "Father, can I pray while smoking?"
The priest glowed, "My son, of course. One can always pray."

I loved the magic of the little story's words, and often repeated it.

As Bob was leading and losing men in the Vietnam jungle,
I was ending my two-year hospital stay.

While I was attending a community college,
he was in Japan recovering from severe battle wounds.

We both married.
He, to Cheryl, his high school love.
Me, to Gina, two months after meeting her.

I became a schoolteacher.
He headed an FBI task force to eliminate the mob.

When my school career ended, I started leading workshops for teachers.
He was being tried by the government for refusing to break the promise he
made to an informant.
He always kept his word…even to a crime boss.
I believed him.
So did the dozens of FBI agents — photographed for the front page of the
New York Times — who were cheering as he entered the courthouse.

He was jailed.

A newspaper did a little article about my life.
His story was featured on 60 Minutes.

Through the years, I often used his parable, with its subtle logic and clever
sequencing, to make a point.

Then, I saw a movie where a character recited it.
It's out there now.
I may not be able to use it anymore.

Bob standing, me not.

Graduating high school from the hospital.

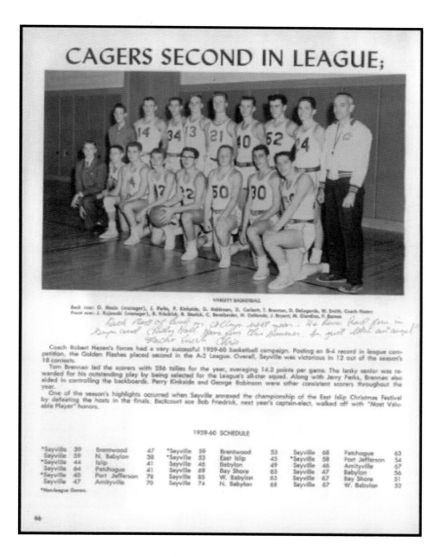

I'm number 4. Bob is to my right.

THE HAND

Uncle Charlie refused to lend my parents $300, so they never bought the rowboat and outboard motor.

The point is not about the foolishness of a struggling couple in the South Bronx trying to buy a boat. Rather, it's that my folks never had any money. We had a roof and food, but there wasn't much of anything in the bank. They both dropped out of school and started working; my mother at Nedick's, my father at Diddy's diner. When they met in their early twenties, they got married. It's what most couples did back then.

We had no rowboat, but we had a car. A used Buick.
During a summer drive we passed a model house.
Parr Homes. Two bedrooms, an unfinished attic, and a plot of land for $6,000. The salesman was given a $20 down payment.
We had a few months to save before the house was built. I guarded the money, hidden in a strongbox kept under my bed. Every few weeks we'd open it, counting up our savings.
It reached a few hundred dollars before the big moving day.
My parents were excited but nervous about leaving the apartment and taking the leap.
My mother got a job in a supermarket and my father bounced around from milkman, to propane truck driver, to bakery deliveries. He was a drinker.
Ronkonkoma didn't have a high school, so I took the bus to Sayville, an affluent town, unlike the one I lived in. The Sayville kids lived in big houses setback far from the street.
Some had pianos in their living rooms.

It was the evening after Thanksgiving when I had my accident. Instead of being a graduating senior, I was a patient in Huntington Hospital. Then, after the surgeries, two years in the State Rehabilitation Hospital at Haverstraw where I was handed my high school diploma from a small, gray-haired lady named Helen Hayes. After investigating my parent's income and discovering that they couldn't afford anything beyond a few token gestures, the doctors and the hospital wrote it up as a loss. At least that's the way I remember it.

After gradually absorbing the depth of my disability, and realizing I'd never be able to do any physical work, and was poorly prepared for mental work, I knew I was in trouble.

The hospital social worker advised me to contact the DVR.

The Division of Vocational Rehabilitation.

It was a New York State program designed for people like me. A representative of the agency, Mr. Lopiparo, came to my house. He was a pleasant and helpful young man. I think of him whenever I see John Turturro, the actor. He explained that since my family had no financial resources beyond a mortgaged house, I could take a test, and if I did well enough, the State would take care of my college expenses. Although I was always disinterested in school, it was the choice I made. Mr. Lopiparo arranged an appointment for me to be evaluated by a psychologist who had me manipulate jig-saw pieces and do some math.

Afterwards, he gave me an oral exam.

One question was, "What would you do if you were lost in the woods?"

I am lost in the woods, I thought.

I answered. "I'd look for the green, mossy side of the trees. That would be North. I'd use that as a directional guide."

I made it up.

I did well enough so that New York would pay for my education.

First Suffolk County Community College, then Adelphi University where I received a bachelor's degree. After academic drifting, I entered a teaching program.

It could provide a destination, a job, a salary.

I met Gina. Got married. Earned a master's degree. Had a house built. Taught a few graduate classes at Adelphi, then was hired by a school district to teach 5th graders. After 34 years,
I retired. Then I applied successfully for a position instructing teachers. Nothing spectacular. Nothing extraordinary. No heroics.

The point of all this is that I've been living a full life, participating in society, traveling, and paying taxes. Actually, I've repaid the State many times over for the help they gave me after becoming a 17-year-old quadriplegic.
I hope some of that tax money goes toward rescuing some kid caught in what appears to be a hopeless situation.

Someone — the unknown, but true hero of this story — suggested that New York State develop a program designed to help people get back on their feet; a program that made a big difference in my life.
Without it, I'm certain my parents would have had to tend to me until they could no longer do so. Eventually, I likely would have been admitted to some institution.

Sometimes, if the government invests in a person, especially one trapped in a difficult spot, it might be the best investment the governmen could ever make.

I received a call the day after this story was printed in Newsday.
It was a woman named Pat. While reading it, she started shaking.
Jerry Lopiparo was her husband. He died years go.
He worked for DVR before becoming a psychologist.
She said he would have been thrilled to know that he helped save a life.

REVOLUTIONS PER MINUTE

We anchored it between our feet while my sister turned the crank.

I'm my own grandpa
I'm my own grandpa
It sounds funny I know
But it reallyy iiss ssoooo…..

The beige Victrola played until the coiled energy was spent, and the song would groan to a funhouse-mirror halt.
We'd try to imitate it.

The brittle record was turned with care.
One slip and it would shatter like porcelain.
We knew about that.
Our hearth was a thick wooden radio. It filled our apartment with crackling songs, and tobacco-colored light.
It became furniture after the TV moved in with Davey Crockett and his theme song.
Each week, the 'Hit Parade' sorted out the top tunes.
"Shrimp boats is a'commin……."
Music was always there spicing moments and backlighting moods.
It was a random soundtrack.
It was simply there, shadowing the main event…my life.
I never pressed rewind.

Dad was strong. Maybe the strongest man in the world.
His scar was from the battle of the Philippines.
He'd toss the ball underhanded to me.

Doctor Green walked up the two landings holding his black leather bag which smelled of assurance.

He would make me better. Always.

Sister Rose Perpetual knew everything. She'd take the long wooden pole and open the classroom window just a bit.
She drilled us on the Catechism and charted our wrongs and rights.
During the Series, she'd chalk the inning and score on the blackboard.
The Dodgers would be heroes if we could only wait.
Maybe just one more year.

Our President made the world wonderful, happy and safe. We were the land of the free and the brave. Everybody knew that.
Stars and Stripes were forever!
I marched out of the Lowes along Willis Avenue with John Phillip Sousa in my head.

Our home cooked meals were eaten to woes about Chinese starvation.
But they weren't starving alone.
I began starving for explanations.

My body was changing and so was the music.
Bird Dog Chain Gang Spanish Harlem

I was seeing the world differently too.
The promise was looking more like a compromise.
Blue Moon was becoming *Bad Moon Rising*.

I started pitching softer to my father.
During an argument, my mother screamed the truth about his scar.
Doctor Green died.
The nuns were found to have said things that were untrue and worse.
The Dodgers stayed in two hotels. One was for blacks.
The White House was the return address for 58,000 caskets filled with Democracy.

He appeared on the Les Crane show. February, '65.

His hair spoke as he howled in dark clothing, scarf orbiting his neck.

The words came out in a rusty growl full of splintered edges.

"It's Alright Ma, I'm Only Bleeding."

"Even the President of the United States must sometime hafta' stand naked."

'California Girls' and all the rest instantly became 'Muzak.'

He barked and wailed songs about injustice.

About barons, and blood on linoleum, and skin torn open by ropes.

All the neat answers became questionable.

He sang, *"The Times, They Are A'Changin."*

And for me, they were.

Me, when I believed what I was told.

BITCH

It was a gift. One I'd have to accept without hedging.

I was suspicious yet intrigued.

She demanded a handshake, which I gave. The verbal contract was made.

There was no backing out. What was I in for?

She handed me the Happy Anniversary card.

Neatly printed was an appointment for a scheduled colonoscopy.

As I read the card, she read my expression.

"No backing out."

Ironic.

Words ending with 'oscopy' are never good. I heard about them.

A tube with an eyeball, peering, as it inches its way through the inner sanctum.

After my pointless refusals were rejected, I slumped the shoulders and swallowed.

What happened to the Age of Aquarius?

I had reached the age of the medical scavenger hunt.

The procedure was wisely scheduled for the week after our trip to the Cape.

Bad test results would certainly spoil our vacation. Better afterward.

We crossed the canal and drove along the bicep of the arm-like peninsula, turned left at the elbow, and on to the fist of Provincetown.

A fist suited this place with its defiance and anything-goes anatomy.

We met two friends at La Luna, where reservations are a must, but reserve is not.

One waiter and one waitress tended the busy tables.

She wore thick black-framed glasses with upturned corners. The type worn by the geek in a made-for-teen movie.

Her black hair was bound in dual, circular buns, one on each side of her head.

And, she had a beard.

Not a few straggly, grandma sow bristles.

It was a two-inch long, flannel-shirt-pass-the-chain-saw beard.

We traded some special of the day Mahi-Mahi Portobello chat.

I navigated through the complex exchange one might encounter when unexpectedly talking with a bearded woman. Somehow, I figured that by whistling past the whiskers, I could safely address the less controversial hair on her head. The wine encouraged me.

I said, "Your hairdo resembles Mouseketeer ears.

She said, "You resemble a wise ass."

This was probably a fair assessment.

I was starting on my salad and enjoying the drive-by conversation with her as she worked the tables.

I asked, "What brought you to P-town?"

That's what you call the place if you want to be considered cool.

I did.

"We're in town to do some shows. We're a two-woman group called 'Bitch and Animal."

The beard had to be a clue.

"Can I call you Animal?"

She laughed and called over to the waiter, who was actually a waitress,

"Hey Animal, he thinks you're Bitch."

Animal laughed too.

Bitch asked me the stock questions.

Where are you from?

What do you do?

Married?

How long?

She poured wine as I answered the questions.

The salads came to the table.

Mine was crowned with a small Bermuda onion ring.

I stared at it.

It reminded me of a sphincter.

I started whining about my upcoming medieval gift, and how I was lured into a women-are-from-Venus flytrap.

Bitch stood still.

Her eyes went fluid.

Sighing, she said, "That's one of the most beautiful things, ever."

She appeared truly touched by the romance of the life-extending gift.

"I have to write a song about this."

Yeah, everyone is in a band, and everyone is going to write a song, I thought.

"Good luck with the song, Bitch," I said, as we were leaving the restaurant.

I grabbed a newspaper at the hotel. The front page had a photo of the duo. Inside was a review of Bitch and Animal.

The cutting edge doesn't get much sharper than this. Two chicks, ten instruments, two tongues that make five more. It's electric violin and African drums. It's tap-shoe ukulele rock. It's hoedown funk poetry. It's bass lines and word rhymes that won't leave your mind.

A rave.

They were doing their final show for the season at Bubala's.

10 p.m. on Saturday.

Bubala's. A classy dive, with twinkling lights and a wooden floor full of stains and stories.

We were offered a large, round, front row table. The place started filling up. Some men, clearly coupled, kissing and touching, but mostly women. A group approached us. They were dressed for Rocky Horror Motorcycle Maintenance. These were real industrial strength lesbians, wrapped in buckled leather, with spikes and piercings, not the variety who are merely going through a phase. There were no little rice-paper umbrellas in their beer bottles.

We shared talk, jokes, and drinks. The table was relaxed.

We were having fun…being loud, laughing… until the lights dimmed.

The show started.

A spotlight haloed Bitch, who was standing at a microphone with an electric violin tucked under her beard.

Animal was off to the right with bongos and congas and other devices.

Silence.

Bitch started singing, 'Twinkle Twinkle Little Star', and, before my eyes could go into a roll, the song exploded into a fantastic chant. What a start!

The songs filled up the hall.

There were anthems and ballads and howls.

Between songs, our table was throwing out instant reviews…

"Wow...Splendid...Unique....Original…"

The drums were primitive energy.

Her hands were a blur as the conga controlled us.

Of course she was Animal.

Bitch started getting warm.

She picked up her guitar and took off her dress.

Down to a shiny white slip and black work boots that went halfway up the calves.

Bitch was working and sweating.

Her body started to glisten from the overhead theatrical lighting.

She had a beautiful, friendly smile, full of straight bright teeth.

Her full breasts were spilling over her bra.

As she got wetter, the slip held to her sensual body.

She was stunning.

She moved and spoke with intoxicating charm.

I was falling for a bearded lesbian.

Well into the show, she grabbed the microphone.

"A very special guest is in the audience tonight. I wrote this next song for him."

Our heads all snapped around looking for the celebrity.

"I call him Colon-Man. You see, his wife loves him so much that she gave him a most precious gift."

She smiled at me.

Everyone followed her eyes in my direction.

Although I enjoyed the attention and recognition, I knew that 'Colon-Man' could have its own local interpretation up here in P-town.

"I wrote this song about her gift to him."

She sang the ballad.

It was warm, slow, full of emotion and mood.

The song, the evening, and Bitch were all beautiful.

A few years later, I came across an ad for a club in the city.

Bitch and Animal would be appearing.

We sat in the dark room as the show began.

After a few hypnotizing songs Bitch started working the violin, but abruptly stopped.

Shading her eyes from the spotlight, she squinted into the audience, and shouted,

"Colon-Man is here!"

JOE

I don't remember how I found out you were dead.
It wasn't the newspaper.
Maybe talk in the neighborhood.
There were no details, just...Joe is dead.

Alphy was working at the Queen's District Attorney's Office.
Detectives had resources...so he'd be able to get the details.
His call came back in an hour.
It happened in Redwood, California.

The door to the rented cottage was ajar. The landlady spotted your false teeth
on the ground, which prevented it from closing.
She also found your body.
The medical examiner counted thirty stab wounds and blunt-force
skull damage
Three men were arrested. One, a known transvestite.
The four of you met in a gay bar, had some drinks, then proceeded to
your place.
The police retrieved the knife. The trial established the cause of the skull
damage...a liquor bottle.

Your wake was on a warm fall night in one of those large lake houses with
broad verandas covered by awnings. Before air-conditioning they catered to
escapees from the city heat. They were now used for year-round businesses...
accounting firms, insurance brokers, and this place...a funeral parlor.
Your father was there, appearing only slightly drunk. He gazed at my crutches,
which were propped against an empty chair. Realizing I was there, he shouted,

"Meatballs! You two are meatballs!"

I said nothing.

I looked straight ahead.

No point. It's over.

You and I never had the chance for a final talk.

Actually, we never managed to have a beginning talk either.

In the silence, I thought about it.

Remember how it started?

I was the kid from the South Bronx who moved into the new house at the end of North Fourth Street; an unpaved, dead-end road.

I walked to where the dirt met blacktop. Victory Drive.

Victory for who?

Johnny was killed in the car accident.

I broke my neck.

Alphy slept while the fire spread.

And you…well, you know.

After sitting on the curb, watching some locals playing stickball, I was invited into the game. They advised to avoid hitting the ball over the high chain-link fence. King, the Great Dane, standing, on the other side. He was big and had a deep bark.

The property had stately trees shading a house with stucco siding and a front porch enclosed by a waist-high half wall. Two concrete tracks led from the street, across the lawn, to a garage set back on the property. It appeared to be the home of wealthy folks.

Back then, I didn't realize that nobody rich would have been living in our neighborhood of modest homes and converted bungalows.

As we played, two kids approached. You were the tall, skinny, one. Your thin brown hair was hanging, partially covering your eyes. You'd snap your head to one side and the hair would move momentarily from your face, only to flop down again. After looking me over, you asked the group,

"Who's the new punk?"

They were the first words I ever heard you say.

"Who's the new punk?"

I was wearing shorts. Nothing on top.
It was summer and I was now a country boy.
You wore pants and a fully buttoned long sleeved shirt.
You eyed me with a sneer.
I avoided fights, and sure didn't want one on my first day in this new place.
You walked toward the fence, opened the gate, pet King, and went into the stucco house.
Our battle came a few days later. I don't remember the cause, but it was more grabbing and pushing than fighting. A primitive ritual, it seemed, that had to occur before becoming best friends. The contact allowed me to feel just how skinny you were. Like tossing around an empty bird cage.
We stayed friends until my sister came down with polio.
All the local parents put out a warning to stay away from me and the disease I might be harboring. There was a panic. Some kids were forbidden to swim in the Lake. People were frightened and theories were common.
The caution passed in a few months when Barbara left the hospital fully recovered, and you and I were back on our bikes doing your newspaper route. I was impressed. You'd knock and say, "Collect." People would pay. Some gave you tips.
You were a businessman.

You were also fun.
It was your idea to catch lightning bugs, keep them in an empty jar, take them to the Ronkonkoma theater, and release them during the movie.
July would come to Lake Ronkonkoma, but you wouldn't. You stayed home. The rest of us lived the long shoeless summers in bathing suits. You didn't say it, but we all knew. You were ashamed... painfully ashamed... of your

boney, pale body. Your summer vacations meant pants and shirts, buttoned from neck to wrist.

You disappeared for the season. Even hiding underneath the clothing embarrassed you. It must have been hell. A five-minute walk away from paradise…a big lake, sliding ponds, a raft with a diving board, a jukebox, baby oil, French fries, busloads of people from places West, and daughters in bikinis. I was too busy with my fun to have considered your pain.

I have regrets. Shooting a squirrel. The chores I rarely did to help my parents. But mostly, the one about you. I teased you about never getting undressed in front of the guys.

"Hey Joe, why don't you get naked in front of us? Maybe you don't have pubic hair?"

You abruptly went into the bathroom and returned moments later, angrily throwing some pubic hair at me. You ran from the house.

I'm sorry about that Joe. I wish I had understood things better…or sooner.

When the summer ended, I was off to public school, and you to Seton Hall, along with your two younger siblings. You wore green uniforms, until your folks ran out of money and you joined me on the bus to Sayville High.

I played on all the teams and you stole books from the library.
I liked the Everly Brothers and you thought Al Jolson was the best.
Kids said, "Al who?"
You liked playing golf on caddy-day.
I said it was for old folks.
We had debates about the limits of the universe, the meaning of life, and which Yankee pitcher had the best pick-off move.
But it always trailed back to religion and God.

You'd say, "The Pope is infallible."

I'd say, "He shits in the woods."

"Oh yeah, well he was given a letter from Our Lady of Fatima. It was about the future of the world. After reading it he fainted."

"Maybe it was the laundry bill from cleaning all his goofy costumes."

I saw religion as a fraud, while it was your bedrock.
Each Sunday you went to services at Saint Joseph's, avoiding the late mass where your father would be. His nose, red and pitted. His eyes, sagging and watery from a hangover.
He handled the wicker collection basket which was mounted on a long pole… the length of a broomstick…so it could reach the mid-pew parishioners.
He spoke like a big shot. He knew everybody. He had pull.

"Mention my name, Charlie."

Even if I was headed to the concession stand at the beach to buy a soda.

"Tell them you know Charlie.."

He pulled up to your house in his Ford sedan and took out a basket of white peaches. Claiming they were a special gift from an important client, he gave one to each of us. They were white all the way through. That's the only pleasant memory I have of him.

"Meatballs!"

Your mother was very sad and very Catholic. Everything about her life was anchored in the Religion. She wanted you to play with Catholic boys… church goers.
She didn't approve of my kind.
It hurt when you told me that she didn't want me, a pagan, in her house.
She said, "I trust him as far as I can throw him."

I didn't quite understand that expression, but I knew it wasn't a compliment.

Didn't she know that you were the guy who did the stealing and lying?

You called the nylon jacket your *thieving wardrobe*.

The flannel lining was torn at the top where you would hide your bounty. It got a lot of use.

We'd go to Royal Scarlet and you'd steal.

Not one cupcake, but five.

Not one Devil Dog but handfuls.

Even things you didn't want and would later throw away.

It made no sense to me.

The shopkeeper knew what you were doing, but could never catch you, even when you swiped the whole lot of TV guides, rack and all. There must have been thirty. What were you thinking? Your lies were like that too. Most of them were pointless and provided no payoff. It appeared to be just theft and lies as a sporting event.

When Fall approached, and clothing was required, you were, like your dog's name, King. You never had the girls, but you sure had everyone else. My mother called you her second son.

The guys all wanted to be in on your adventures. Me too.

Although I wanted no part of the crazy ones, I joined in. You led us to the abandoned Vanderbilt Mansion at the end of Motor Parkway. We followed your lead in jumping off the ballroom balcony into a pile of old mattresses collected from the long-ago deserted bedrooms.

I hated doing it.

Winter meant throwing snowballs at cars. I wouldn't throw, but I ran away with you.

You could have hurt people.

And we could have caught a well-deserved beating.

I just couldn't enter the underground fort you dug out of the hard ground.
It was big enough to hold six. I pictured the earth collapsing and all of you
suffocating. Would I be able to dig you out with my hands?
It seemed like forever that you'd be down there while I'd be shooting baskets
by myself.

When Ronkonkoma was frozen over, you'd gather the crew to take night
expeditions across, rather than around, the Lake. We'd reach the middle
where the winds would howl. You'd jump up and down making the ice crack.
Begging you to stop, we'd hear the sound of the groaning
ice-fault as it radiated away from us. We had no idea how close we were to
death on those evenings, although, looking back, I think you did. You might
have even wanted the ice to fail and swallow us all together.
Or maybe you thought your God would protect us.
Yes, we always made it into town on the other side, and we got through our
teenage years.
All, except for Johnny.
His parents sold the cottage right after the car accident.

But things were changing.
You quit school and went away.
And you know what happened to me.
Two years in a hospital.
Then, college.
Me. College!
Then marriage.
I would have asked you to be my best man if I knew where you were.
Alphy took your place.

Your two older brothers were never around. I only saw the redhead once in
all those years, and, after the blonde got shot, he also vanished.

Your sister too. She disappeared. It was right after she farted while throwing the football in front of all the guys. I never saw her again. I figured that she became a nun.

Your younger brother was a little version of you, although not as pale, and hardly as skinny.
He had one eye that drifted off.
I ran into him twice. The first time, he swore he'd soon be the next James Dean. He was certain. He was still living with your parents but hadn't said a word to your father in years. He had his own fork, knife, and plate so he'd never have to use one your father touched.
The last time we met, he claimed to have given up all earthly things.
He was wearing a brown robe and trying to re-live the life of Christ.

It seemed everyone escaped from your father, his liquor, and the temper I only heard about.

People said Charlie had lost his job.

You stole a copy of Death of a Salesman from the library, urging me to read it. I did.
Looking back, I think you were trying to tell me something.
I saw your family as I read that play.
I still do.

While speaking, you had taken to covering your mouth with your hand. I knew that you were hiding your decaying teeth. Oddly, your mother started confiding in me. She told me that, once, when you were drunk and sleeping on the couch, she lifted your lip and saw that your teeth were rotted out. I disliked sharing in this personal invasion of your privacy.
You moved from job to job.
You did some work as a short-order cook where you met Harriet.
You called and asked if I'd be your best man.

"Of course."

You never gave me the date or location of the wedding.

It must have been two years later, you called.

"Me and Harriet, are going to stop by your place tonight."

We'd finally get to meet her.
You showed up alone, claiming she, at the last minute, had to cover for a waitress at the diner.
I was beginning to think that she never existed. I never got to find out, because you 'divorced' her.

You decided to join the Army.
Before the paperwork was arranged, you lost your right index finger — your trigger finger —in the machine shop accident, and feared rejection from the military.
More rejection.
But the United States Army sent you and your nine fingers to Vietnam. You were gone for a long time. In a way, you never returned.

My mother called to tell me that her house had been burglarized. No money was taken. Just clothes and underwear. She was upset. Would I come over? As I turned right off Victory to the dead-end street, I saw someone running past the old doghouse that King used to sleep in.
I was sure it was you.
The rumor was, that although you had been home for a few months, you'd been in seclusion. I called and talked you into visiting the next day. It was just the two of us. You were no longer hiding behind your hand; the army fitted you with false teeth. After reliving old times, you said you had something to tell me. You wrote it on a piece of paper, put it on the table across the room,

and left. By the time I got to the note you were halfway down the dead-end street. It said,

"I love you."

From that point on it was appear and disappear. You'd visit for an evening then be gone for months. Sometimes years. After serving jail time for stealing a car, you were at our door. You explained, true-to-Hollywood formula, that a black inmate sodomized you.
I asked you about God. Was your faith still solid after all the things you've been through.

"Yeah, it's solid."

Then, you were gone once again, as was some of Gina's clothing. A year later, during the very last visit, you told me about the fun you were having. In the evenings, you'd dress up as a woman, go out drinking, and have lots of laughs. I did my best to not be shocked. I didn't realize we were having our final conversation, although I remember that last question I asked you.

Your mother called. First time ever.

"Hello Bruce, this is Joseph's mother. How are you?"

"Oh, hello. Fine. Thanks. How are you?"

"Well, I'm just concerned about Joseph. Have you two spoken recently?"

"He stopped by a few weeks ago. Sure, we chatted."

"Did he mention anything about what he's been up to?"

Neither of us was sure of what the other knew. We inched our way into the conversation.

"He told me that he goes out at nights and has fun," I answered.

"Did he mention anything about his clothing?"

I was starting to think that she knew at least as much as I did.

"Yes…he mentioned how he dresses up."

She was reaching the same conclusion about me. That I knew.

Trying to maintain her composure, she said,

"Well, he walks around the house in a bra and panties. It's killing me to see him that way. He goes out to bars dressed as a woman. He sees nothing wrong with it. I think he's trying to punish me."

Then, she added,

"If he must do it, I wish he'd dress more conservatively and not so trashy. Some nights he looks quite presentable, but other nights…"

She asked if Gina or my mother were missing clothing.

"Yes. They both are. Missing clothing and wigs."

"I think Joseph borrowed them. How can I get the property back to you?"

"Oh please, just discard everything."

"Are you sure? It's no problem…"

"Yes. Just discard it all."

Joe, I think about our final conversation, and the question I asked you.

"After all you've been through Joe, do you still believe in God?"

"Yes. But I don't like him anymore."

FINGERS

Along with the warm weather came Alphy and Johnny.

They summered at the bungalow with their mother, while their father continued his detective work in the city.

He'd be there on the weekends, mostly to play golf, barbecue, or to varnish his wooden picnic table. It reflected like fine furniture.

The three of us were too young to drive, so we entertained ourselves with the Lake on sunny days. Rain meant the Ronkonkoma Theater, or maybe solving the mysteries of the universe from someone's porch.

In the evenings we'd go to Turner's Park...our Brigadoon...which came to life every May. Long trucks would congregate, unload contraptions, poles, boards, steel frames, wires, canvas and men.

And, within days, there it was—a little Coney Island.

The place had rides, and games of chance. We never had luck winning a glass bowl or a stuffed animal. The people who worked there were carnival folks… con artists, barkers, and hustlers,

all with strange looks. When Turner's Park disappeared in September, so did the 'carnies.'

Some nights meant Lakeside Miniature Golf. Two guys, both named 'Freddy,' worked there. Old Freddy, and Fingerless Freddy. We called him Fingerless Freddy even though he had eight. The word was that he lost a pair to fireworks. I saw him as a grotesque and incomplete human.

Deliberately avoiding any contact with him, I made sure to order potato chips from Old Freddy. From the back of the concession stand Fingerless said,

"I got it. Here you go. Twenty-five cents please."

"Thanks."

I took the bag from him, being most careful to avoid handling the contaminated spot, while trying not to hurt his feelings.

I walked to the side of the concession stand where he couldn't see me drop it into the trash can.

Fall approached and Alfie and Johnny returned to the city. After having the accident, I found myself in a hospital rehabilitation ward with some twenty men and boys with assorted and serious disabilities.

I soon learned that on most weekday evenings local volunteer women in peppermint-stripped dresses and disciplined smiles, came to offer the patients help if we needed it.

Mail a letter. Buy a comb. Pick up a newspaper.

Boots Passamonte, who lost significant function after his drunk-driving accident, asked for another bottle of Vitalis.

He used a lot of Vitalis.

The ladies became suspicious and soon discovered that he had been drinking the hair lotion for its alcohol content despite the biting taste.

One of the ladies — wealthy looking, middle aged, attractive, and thick with makeup — offered to purchase sandwiches for the ward.

I put my order in.

When she returned, she delivered the sandwiches to each of the patients who were laying in beds or sitting in wheelchairs.

She put the sandwich next to my shoulder.

I struggled to handle it.

An old, legless patient in a wheelchair, saw my difficulty. He rolled over and offered help.

I couldn't get, "No thanks," out fast enough.

As he unwrapped the sandwich, I noticed his fingertips were missing.

Cut off, burned off, frozen off?

Bent, twisted nails were growing from the stumps.

He held the sandwich.

I stretched to bite an untouched corner.

"Thank you. That's enough for me tonight."

I discarded it the next day.

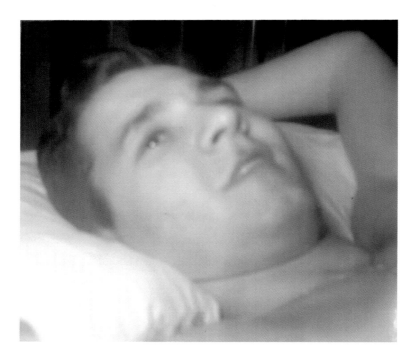

Me, paralyzed from the neck down.

FLASH

Even after he became an adult, I called him Stevie.

We were baseball loving cousins.

He was born three years after me, so I had the physical advantage that some thousand days provide at that age.

Our fathers were brothers.

Uncle Gene's family lived in a third-floor apartment on 144th.

We lived on Willis Avenue, four blocks away.

Gene was a cop stationed in the 40th precinct. He could have walked to work.

My father was a cook at Diddy's Diner.

Our parents developed issues. Something they called a 'falling out,' so I didn't get to see Stevie much.

A local punk named Warren made the *Daily News* after being shot to death by a zip gun. Another kid was shot dead within weeks.

The neighborhood was changing. Something a cop might have sensed early.

So, Gene, Aida, Stevie and his younger brother moved to Cambria Heights.

It was like country, with trees along the sidewalk, and each compact brick house with a small plot of grass the size of a living room carpet.

We too, soon left the South Bronx.

Ronkonkoma had trees everywhere.

And, a big lake.

Being kids, we didn't know the details, but were glad when our parents reconciled.

I spent that summer in Cambria Heights playing baseball with Stevie's team… the Tigers. Gene was the manager, and our games were planned around his police shifts. He'd strap on his shoulder holster and go off to work in the morning, no longer wearing a uniform after being promoted to detective.

He came home to meat and potatoes every night.

On nice days Stevie and I would swim in the inflated backyard pool. Occasionally we'd invite our way into the neighbor's inground.

We ate tons of tomato sandwiches on white bread, and of course, we played baseball.

On a sunny afternoon we were throwing a ball around when she walked by. Joann Nicolosi.
It was the first time I ever had that feeling.
They say it's like having the breath taken away.
They're right... because that's what it felt like.
Even today I could point to that spot where she stood.
Stevie sensed something happening to his older cousin...uncertain just what it was.
We were growing up.
Me, just a little bit sooner.

A few years later, I had my accident and Stevie joined the military and got a tattoo.
After the hospital, I went to college, mostly by default.
Stevie developed an ear problem, was granted a military discharge, and joined the police force.
Following his father, he requested an assignment in the same precinct.
He had a connection and knew the neighborhood.
He wore his father's badge.

The Mott Haven section of the Bronx had changed again.
The blacks and Puerto Ricans were displaced by immigrants from the Islands and Central America.
While it was not the notorious precinct known as Fort Apache, the locals called it 'The Baddest Station in the Nation.'

I was almost finished with school when my breath was taken away again. Gina.

I got married.

Stevie had women in his life.

And then he met Lorraine.

He was finally grounded. With a good wife and a hefty baby with red hair who could shake his playpen like a Sumo wrestler.

We hardly ever saw each other.

No issues.

Just life.

My father died. Lung cancer.

Years of cigarettes.

Uncle Gene died. Emphysema.

Years of cigarettes.

I wanted to show Gina my old neighborhood, so we crossed the Willis Avenue Bridge.

The bedroom window where I looked out at my world.

Saint Pius School, where I learned to read.

Saint Mary's Park, where I was a diver.

Barney's candy store, now a bodega.

143rd, where the stonecutters worked and where I played stickball.

There were few cars parked on the street.

They were too much of a luxury for the neighborhood.

Seeing a squad car by the corner, I made sure to stop before the light went red.

I looked over at the driver who had a cigarette hanging from his mouth.

He turned and gave a glare.

It quickly turned to a smile as Stevie jumped out of the car.

He explained that his hard look was a result of our white faces…something rarely seen in Mott Haven, other than on out-of-towners looking to buy drugs or rent a prostitute.

He had a name tag above his badge…FLASH.

During our curbside reunion, locals walked by and shouted out…

"Hey Flash."

"Flash, my man."

"Yo, Flash."

He seemed to be a local hero.

I retired from teaching and did some subbing.

He retired from the force, and started a business selling shirts and jackets at the precinct.

Each item bore the words…The Baddest Station in the Nation.

He missed the guys and the old brick building.

We'd talk a few times a year by phone.

He'd occasionally send a letter, usually with a newspaper clipping about the Bronx.

But the Christmas card came every year.

I could pick his out from the others by the beautiful handwriting.

It was always addressed, To Igor and Bella, from Taras and Natasha.

He liked reminding me of our Ukrainian heritage.

Even after he came down with the breathing issue, we'd be sure to get that Christmas card every December.

Sometimes our phone conversations ended abruptly.

He'd start choking.

He needed to use his nebulizer.

His throat would fill up.

He finally gave up cigarettes, on most days.

Christmas came. But no card.

Lorraine made the call to us.

The next day a letter arrived, addressed to Igor and Bella, from Taras and Natasha.

Sharing a bat with Stevie.

Stevie hatless.

Stevie, in front of his precinct house.

The girl in the fuzzy pink sweater and tight beige jeans.

FREDDY'S SHIRT

In 1973, the Dow Jones was hitting the mid 800's, and gas was 40 cents a gallon.

The Vietnam War was winding down and the Trade Center became the World's tallest building. The barcode was changing shopping, and, in the evenings, folks were watching the Partridge Family, but only if they were in front of the TV at the right time.

I was starting my seventh year of teaching.

Twenty seven scrubbed kids entered "The Thinking Laboratory" — room 104 — at Norwood School.

One of the boys had freckles, a tossed-salad head of curly red hair, and a wide smile. Freddy.

The smile was to last the whole year. He constantly shared it and it spread like a happy virus in the classroom.

He was an average student but not an average person.

With the rare balance of wonder, fun, and compassion, he approached each day with focused excitement. I once told him that he blinked faster than most people because he didn't want to miss a bit of life.

The school year was a productive pleasure, much of it because of Freddy. He would laugh the loudest when playing and be the saddest over anyone's misfortune.

As June approached, I wanted to leave these fifth-graders with a special gift. I drew a picture of myself under a slogan, *Verbs Are Your Friends*. A company made the shirts in assorted sizes. I passed them out and we hugged goodbye.

Through the years I'd run into former students who would provide updates on their old classmates. One told me that Freddy was a communications specialist in the Navy. A few years later I learned that Freddy became an avid fisherman who'd travel to anyplace that had water. He spent every October at a remote part of Maine, living the rough life.

I heard how he gave the little money he saved up to a fellow worker whose kids needed help.

Someone told me how Freddy helped out homeless people however he could.

It was no surprise that he grew up to be the same caring person I met forty years before.

I was teaching a workshop at Stony Brook University when there was a knock at the door.

A woman, excusing the interruption, entered and handed me a bulky manila envelope.

Curious, I stopped teaching and opened it.

There was the shirt. Old but intact.

The note from his mother said,

"Freddy developed Diabetes at age thirty. It made him weak and thin.
Insulin stabilized him and he continued with his active, hard working life.
Until, a few years later, his body started developing internal tumors.
They grew in places which were inoperable.
He seemed fine until he fell through the shower door.
The doctors suspected it was sinus.
After returning home from one of his Maine adventures with his father,
the second fall brought him to the hospital.
A tumor was strangling his lungs.

There was nothing the doctors could do.
Freddy died on Thanksgiving.

He would have wanted you to have this."

Love
Kitty

The returned shirt.

Freddy, thumbs up optimist.

DOMINICANS

The first was Rhadames Batista. He was a stocky ten-year-old who came from the Dominican Republic, which he always referred to as, "My country." He had the assured smile and confidence of an adult, and seemed to be a little man. As I was teaching him fractions, he was teaching me how to eat sugar cane after hacking it with a machete.

It was easy to spot his house, a few blocks from the school.

The front yard was lush with crops and tobacco.

His father wouldn't waste valuable land on a useless lawn.

Each year brought more Dominicans to the school. Families were helping others — relatives, neighbors, and friends — to get here. Many came from the same area...Santiago.

Some kids Americanized their names. Others, like Rhadames, stayed traditional.

Most of the students had attended school back on the Island. A few came from deep rural areas and had no prior schooling or experience with teachers, like the little girl who looked at me with great suspicion.

Some spoke English, and the ones who didn't, picked it up quickly. All were bilingual by the end of the semester.

Raphaela Carravetta, the ESL teacher, helped the kids with language skills, but so much more. An immigrant herself, and a compassionate person by nature, she was a dedicated advocate for the emerging Dominican community.

When it was parent-teacher conference time, the mothers came in while the fathers were working. Many of the kids sat in on the conferences to translate. If a female student teacher participated, she'd likely be surprised by a hug and kiss from a mother. It's a warm culture.

The word that always came up, much more than grades, was respect.

Respect was most important.

"Es mi hijo respetuoso?"

Happily, the answer was always positive. Without exception.
Near retirement, I took a winter trip to Santiago, both, for the weather and
to see a bit of the world these fine kids came from.

They're now parents and grandparents.
Teachers, doctors, scientists, police officers, clerks, business owners,
psychologists…people.

That group of beautiful sisters from one family, are still beautiful, married,
and cherishing handsome children…respectful, I'm sure.
The little girl who was so suspicious, is now a mother and officer in the
U.S. Navy.

Rhadames became a lawyer in Miami.
He called me one night to let me know that his son was born.
He named him Bruce.

Rhadames with baby Bruce.

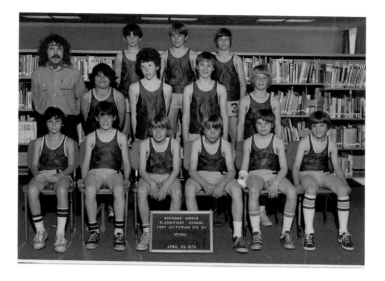

The Snorewood Spuds. Me touching shoulders with Rhadammes.

Raphaela Carravetta, friend and advocate for good people

HAROLD'S BOOK

Edith escorted Harold to the table, securing his steps, before leaving.

We sat under the oak trees.

Edith worked one classroom away.

Shiny silver hair, cut with fashion, and tailored suits set her apart from the younger faculty members. Although separated by wisdom, wealth, and decades, we were friends.

She offered her home overlooking Conscience Bay to host the end of the year party, and, we were to discover later, her uncelebrated retirement. It was there I met Harold. He too, had silver hair, but his was bound into a ponytail. The pledge was that it would remain as long as American soldiers were in Vietnam.

Harold always offered humility and a smile. Unless asked, he didn't talk about himself. The biography came from others, and in pieces.

I learned parts from his daughters, Peggy and Barbara, whenever they were home for a visit and sharing family stories.

More came during the dinners and gatherings at the Friedman's, where friends were given the only drink Harold ever served…Bloody Captains, bed-rocked on 150 proof Demerara Rum, and accented with innocent flavors. He spooned the tempting sherbet-like slosh from a large lab beaker, filling and refilling each glass. As people relaxed so did the talk.

After he graduated from the University of Chicago with an advanced degree, they moved to Los Alamos where he continued his work and they started their family.

Hints of another World War were brewing.

Los Alamos.

I only knew one thing about that place.

Harold was an expert. He knew the secrets of water…heavy water…which he shared with the teams of scientists.

A few names jumped out of the conversations.

Teller.

Oppenheimer.

Others.

After the war, Harold went on to Stony Brook University, sometimes teaching from his own book...*A Course In Statistical Mechanics*...
the study of thermodynamic properties of fluids with applications in oceanography and physiology.
He laughed when I suggested that I'd wait until the movie was released.

On those occasional winter days when I needed a ride to work and Harold couldn't reach the lab by plowing his bike through snow, they'd pick me up in the heater-less VW.
Edith would complain that it was time they bought a new car. One with a deluxe option...an operating heater. Harold, ever smiling, would say,

"Nonsense. Cold is good for the gonads."

We'd laugh as warm smoke rose from our words.
The car was cold, but the house wasn't. It had a glowing fireplace fed with logs cut with the two-man saw.
Harold would say,

"Logs heat twice. Once when you burn them and once when you cut them."

Edith was assigned one end.

During low tide, he'd gather mussels, which were cleaned in the beard-removing device he created. He said he'd get it patented someday. He never did, but we kept eating mussels.

The six-way conversation with the Taubs, their other Sunday breakfast guests, was about food, good recipes, and bird feeders.

No one mentioned that Henry was awarded the Nobel Prize in chemistry only a week before.

It was like that with Edith and Harold.

What was to be our last dinner together, Harold had difficulty walking in, but upon reaching his seat, said, "I really need a beer."

The waiter said that Coors was the only option. Harold refused to order it, saying that the Coors Company had an ugly policy toward labor.

Knowing how badly he wanted a beer, I promised that if he ordered one, I'd write a critical letter to the company. He did and I did.

The disease was battering him. We talked about birds and fresh apples, I asked him if he missed his lab?

"Yes."

We heard the crunch of Edith's tires on the gravel.

"Harold, do you ever pick up your book about water and read it?"

With his head hanging low, and in a worn voice he answered. "Yes. But I don't understand it anymore.

I NEVER MET WILLIE SUTTON

Before living color, remotes, or flat screens.
Before Tony Soprano, Kojak, or the Untouchables, we watched Gang Busters.
The weekly TV program reenacted case histories from the open files of law
enforcement. Viewers paying attention to the details, sometimes called the
authorities to offer a tip about
a fugitive.
Gang Busters claimed credit for many apprehensions.
The show presented clues about the F.B.I.'s most-wanted criminals.
Baby-Face Nelson, Ma Barker, John Dillinger.
But to me, no one compared to Willie Sutton.
Willie 'the actor' Sutton.
He got the nickname because of his talent at executing robberies while dis-
guised, maybe as a priest, a grandma, a policeman, or a plumber.
Although he carried a gun, it was always unloaded. He claimed he'd never
want to hurt anyone.
The show often seemed to be about him.
Maybe because he robbed so many banks.
Or because he was caught and imprisoned five times.
But probably because of his escapes.
With his eight-grade education he repeatedly outwitted his jailers.
In one episode he reshaped a bar of soap to resemble a gun, covered it with
shoe polish, and forced a guard into the cell as he escaped.

The actor who played his part resembled Willie. He too, was slight, with
innocent, hanging eyelids, a creased face, and a simple stroke of a mustache.
Like Willie, he'd always be talking and chain-smoking Bull Durhams.

The host of the show explained that this actor was cast because the likeness
might assist in a capture.

During his thirty-year career he robbed millions, when millions were real money. He famously said, "I steal from the rich and keep it."

In 1933 Sutton pulled a job at the Corn Exchange Bank and Trust Company in Philadelphia. He entered disguised as a mailman, but an alert passerby foiled the crime. Sutton fled.

Months later he broke into the same bank through a skylight. This time he was apprehended and sentenced to serve 5 to 50 years in the State Penitentiary. Sutton escaped that institution through a tunnel.

Back in business, he conducted a daylight jewel heist by impersonating a telegram messenger.

Caught, he was sentenced to life as a four-time offender.

He was transferred to a high security prison. Dressed as a guard, he carried two ladders across the yard at night. When the tower spotlight hit him, he yelled, "It's all right."

Another escape.

There were a few more bank jobs, but again, and for a fifth time, he was captured and imprisoned. He couldn't escape.

However, after nearly half a life behind bars, a series of decisions by the U.S. Supreme Court resulted in his release.

In ill health from emphysema and in need of an operation on his leg arteries, the newspaper explained that he was admitted to a New York hospital.

I called, expecting that maybe a nurse or attendant would pass on the good wishes to my childhood anti-hero.

"Hello, I'm calling to see how Mr. Sutton is doing."

"Hold on please."

"Hello."

"Yes. I'm calling to see how Mr. Sutton is doing."

"I'm doing ok."

" Am I actually speaking to Willy?"

"Yeah. I'm me."

It was.
I was talking to him.
The clever criminal who outwitted the law.
The man who robbed banks without ever hurting anyone.
The man who once escaped a prison in a laundry basket,

"How are you?"

"I've got a problem with my legs. They're gonna' cut me soon."

"I'm sure it'll work out ok."

"Well, will see. Maybe I'll escape."

We laughed.

"I used to watch the Gang Busters. You were my favorite always. Duke Snider, Willie Mays, and you were my heroes."

"You got two Willies there."
"I never thought about that."

"You got the Willies."

More laughter.

"The actor looked so much like you."

"Yeah, except I was better looking."

This time his laughter turned to a cough.
He was short of breath.
I thought of the Bull Durhams.

Before ending the call, I asked

"Would you mind if I came in to visit you?"

"Hey, that would be real nice. I don't have much in the way of family.
I'd enjoy the company."

Great.
Willie was gone before I got there.

OPERATION EGG DROP

It was 1969. Grumman Aircraft was commissioned to design the lunar landing module; a device that would deliver astronauts with a soft landing on the Moon.

Several kids in my 5th grade class knew details.
Their parents…mostly fathers… were working on the project. Maybe a radar screen, a heating pipe, a bolt.
Thousands were involved.
We read about problems the Company was encountering.
The fifth graders decided to take up a similar challenge; design and build their own soft-landing devices.
Realizing that they couldn't use people, and it would be too risky for animals, the vote went for eggs.

Fragile, delicate…raw eggs, which the kids called *eggstronuts.*
The task was to build a module with an egg on board that could safely survive an extreme drop-test.

Within weeks the models started coming in and the trials began.

They were tossed from the roof of the two-story school. Most eggs made it. Some failed and were retooled until all passed the test.

But that challenge wasn't adequate.
We needed height. Something lacking on flat Long Island.
The City. The Empire State Building? The Chrysler Building? Police permits. Insurance. Wind. Traffic.
No and No.

MacArthur Airport!
Of course.

The terminal wasn't high, but they had small planes, and pilots.

We were directed to Tom, the flight instructor, who had just landed his Piper Cub.
It didn't take long to convince him.
He smiled and said he'd find two more willing pilots.
We'd just have to pay for the aviation fuel.
We set a date, which gave the kids a few weeks to perfect their modules.
Some openly discussed their plans in class.
Others treated it as a high-level, classified, top-secret.

Alpha day arrived. Kids came to class with amazing devices made of water bags, hacksaw blades, cardboard tubes, rubber bands, pieces of tires, fabrics.
One was a spider web of string suspended on a steel frame which supported a 'floating' egg.
The parents all permitted their kid to participate, and
several helped with the transport.
We parked near the launchpad.
Three Cessnas would make runs, each carrying a pilot and three kids, renamed a 'copilot' and two launchers.
The co-pilot, sitting to the pilot's right, was assigned altimeter duty.
The two launchers took the rear seats.
Each plane rumbled along the concrete runway and cleared the surrounding oak trees, heading toward the school at a steady 2,000 feet.

Upon approach, the pilot shouted, "Open doors."
The pilot and copilot pushed the doors open against the 120 mile per hour wind resistance. Then the pilot ordered, "Release modules."
The launchers shoved the devices out. They tumbled, growing smaller, as the plane banked and headed back to the airport.
When all runs were finished, we returned to the school to retrieve our devices on the seven-acre playground.

A few landed in backyards and were promptly delivered to the school by cooperative neighbors who had heard about the experiment.

One parent contacted Newsday who ran a story about our project, calling it, "Operation Egg-Drop."

The paper reported that all but one of the modules survived, and one was never found.

It's still out there, somewhere.

The paper disclosed that the one failure was designed by a parent — a Grumman engineer — who was certain that it would be the only survivor from the estimated 250-mile per hour collision with the ground.

The class wrote a letter to Grumman offering engineering advice.

They never heard back.

Operation Egg Drop.

KNUCKLES

In 1970, when I was a second-year teacher, my class had a dog.
His name was Knuckles.
He belonged to Eric.

It started on the first day.
The kids were freshly washed, dressed, and excitedly waiting to come into their new classroom.

The room had two doors; an interior hallway door, and another, which opened to an outside courtyard.
The hallway door was mostly used by students who came by bus or biked.
Back then, the school had several bike racks, and they were always filled. The late comers left their bikes resting on the lawn.

The kids who walked to school usually cut across the seven acre playground and entered class through the courtyard.

Eric was a walker.
Knuckles followed him, probably not sensing that Summer was over.

After the kids entered, it just didn't seem right to leave Knuckles outside and alone.
So, I invited him in.
Everyone was excited with normal first day energy, plus having a dog in class.

The kids gave him water, some of their lunch snacks, and took turns petting him.
He got lots of attention.
No one wheezed, so we let him remain in class until dismissal.

Knuckles came back with Eric the next day.
And the next.

And the next.

And every day.

He'd sit at the door, waiting.

If he got impatient, he'd jump up and scratch his paws against the frosty Plexiglass window to alert us that he was there and ready for school, even if Eric was still crossing the playground.

Knuckles always used the courtyard door because we couldn't have a dog walking through the hallways.

After a few weeks, the excitement of having Knuckles wore down.

He was just our class dog.

On one amazing day, Eric was absent, but Knuckles scratched at the window and entered the class.

That convinced us for sure that he was one of us.

He ate treats kids donated from their lunchboxes;

mostly peanut butter and jelly sandwich crusts.

Peanut butter was allowed in school back then.

When Knuckles started making circles or yelping, we'd open the courtyard door

and he'd relieve himself by the brick wall.

During Gym, Music, or Art, we'd close the hallway door and Knuckles would sleep.

He wasn't welcome at assemblies either.

The year went pretty much that way.

During the Spring, it was time for class pictures.

The kids came to school all combed-up.

The photographer lined them up according to height.

They wanted Knuckles to be in the picture.
I said,

"Absolutely not! I refuse to have a naked dog in the picture."

Robert shouted,

"He can wear my tie. He won't be naked!"

"Well, ok. As long as he's wearing a tie."

Knuckles joined us in the picture.
Being the shortest in the class, the kids decided to put him in the front row, next to Eric.

That's how the year went.

One day Knuckles didn't show up at our door.
When Eric entered the class alone, crying, we all knew.

Knuckles. Front row wearing tie, no pants.

JOEL

The "Hello" was meant for me.
I responded with a courteous, "Hi," pretending to know the stranger.
He mockingly commented about his missing hair while moving closer.
I recognized the voice before the face.
My second, "Hi," made the first one sound insincere — shallow.
It was Joel, and he was alive.

I said, "You look great."
It was a polite reflex, spoken without enthusiasm.
I thought, *You look different.*
He saw the questions on my face and started explaining the brutal treatments
that were to make him well.
He must have explained it so often, it came out like a phone solicitation.
While trying to listen, I drifted away… thinking about the last time I saw him.

It was a cold night and he was moving toward the theater, draped like a sagging rope between his cane and Rhoda's shoulder.

They were always together.
But not after that night.
I started seeing her without him.
Maybe she was walking on the beach.
Or leaving a restaurant with a group of women.
He was most noticeable by his absence.

As I came back to his voice, I thought,
So, the last time I saw you was not to be the last time.
There was a swollen fullness that pushed some of the years out of his face,
and he had enough hair left to cover the thinning.

"You really look great."

This time I meant it.

I could have said, "You look alive."

This conversation was like the few others we had, spread out over some forty years…brief and scattered.

We never had a sit-down talk over coffee.

It never seemed worth looking for two chairs.

We quickly agreed that society was falling apart.

He said he doesn't go to the movies anymore.

"They're all the same. Bombs and explosions."

"Well, it's become more about money and…"

"It's always been about money!" he scolded.

"Yes, but it used to be about adult money. Now it's geared for young males who…"

"Want garbage," he finished my sentence.

"But there are still some fine movies like, *No Country for Old Men*.

He offered a weak nod of charitable approval, while I considered the title's irony.

"What about *Match Point*? It was an excellent movie."

"It was too contrived… when the character throws the ring, and it hits the railing…too contrived."

"But life is like that. Outcomes are changed by a second or an inch.
Just think, you and I triumphed over millions of other sperm cells. If we hadn't won the race to…"

"You're an idiot."

"But you didn't let me finish."

"I don't let idiots finish."

I laughed. Laughed hard.
He laughed, too.

ANDY

The call came at night. The words were a scramble of Spanish and English. The phone was passed to different excited voices. None were understandable.

Then, "My Andy my Andy he hurt."

"What? What happened. Who…"

Andy's voice came through the phone. He was crying.
He explained how it happened. The last day of school. He and a friend decided to take the shortcut through the hole in the fence.
They'd fool with the train, then run across the tracks, just in time.
The friend made it.
Andy tripped.
The wheels crossed both thighs.

I wanted to offer a summer escape for two boys who lived in the building I called home in the 50's.
There was no response to my letter. Maybe the apartment building still had no superintendent, just like when I lived there. Or, if there was one now, he'd likely struggle with the language. Either way, it must have been discarded.

I remembered the South Bronx summers. Windows were left open, promising this thing called cross ventilation. It did little to drain the exhausting heat from our four rooms. Air conditioning was decades and dollars away. There was no relief.

Occasionally, some daring renegade would appear with a big wrench and nervously unlock a hydrant. Word would spread. I'd join the crowd spilling out of the tenements, onto the street to get blasted by the cool white force. Screaming joy, until the cops came with a bigger wrench.

The only other break from the swelter was a visit to Uncle Charlie's. Those rare weekends took me away from the baked dryness of Willis Avenue.
His Peekskill home was shaded by thick trees. I'd roll down the sloping lawn of sweet grass. I could smell the Zinnia garden and tomatoes from the porch.
The rabbits smelled them too. My Uncle fired his shotgun into the air to scare them away. At least for a while.
The two hunting beagles trotted along next to us as we took the wooded path leading to the spring-fed pond.
Aunt Lillian gave me cold glasses of buttermilk with lunch.

Two boys could have a summer escape at my country house.
It would be ideal if they were the age I was back then — maybe eleven — and, if they didn't live at 362, at least nearby.

A friend said I was crazy to invite ghetto kids to my home.

"They'll know where you live."

His warning made me more intent.

The closest the operator could get was 366 — a pharmacy.
The druggist spoke little English.

"Yes. Nice…but I don't be involved. Good luck."

I mentioned the idea to my cousin Stevie, a cop in the Mott Haven Precinct.
He knew most of the neighborhood kids.

"I'll pick out two nice boys and drive them out to your house."

His note read, h/m 12 and b/m 12.
It took a while to figure out that our guests would be a Hispanic male and a black male. Both 12.

The kids would have the chance to escape the heat and horrors of 'Hot Haven' and spend a safe week under Setauket trees.

Stevie dropped them off as arranged. Each used a brown paper bag as luggage. My cousin phoned the following day, warning that he found roaches in his trunk.

They enjoyed themselves, sharing the bedroom and bathroom. Going to restaurants and movies. Playing miniature golf, hiking, and swimming.

Andy asked,

"Bruce, how can I get to live like you when I grow up?"

"I'm not sure Andy. Just do the best you can in school. That should help."

The boys cut down a sapling. They walked about in the woods with the dog. They filled the birdbaths and splashed in the Long Island Sound.
Neither had a father. Andy had an older brother. 16 and serving time for armed robbery.

Andy ordered a steak at the all-you-can-eat buffet.
He asked more than once,

"Anything? All I want?"

The waiter put the plate in front of him. Andy held the steak in his left hand and, holding the knife in his right, carved the meat as if whittling a block of wood.
I was certain that he never cut a piece of meat before.
Surely not steak.

Gina took the boys to the mall to buy them clothing.
The week came to a close and we drove them back to the Bronx.

Andy asked again how he could live like us. My weak answer was "education."

We never heard from Lance again, but Andy wrote letters.
Very poorly written letters.
There was an occasional phone call when Andy was near a payphone and had the money.

We'd have Andy out again.
Maybe next summer.
Right after school.

Sister Barbara, beagle, and me at Uncle Charlie's home in Peekskill.

JUSTIN AND URANUS

~A true story from my classroom~

Justin was short and thin, with curly blond hair. Adorable.
He often caused distractions yet managed to stay away from serious trouble because knew where the edges were and that's where he functioned.
He enjoyed the attention of the class, which often came his way. He was popular.
Although the smallest student, he had a street-smart way about him.

Unlike a typical day, where he would be detached from, or just slightly engaged in the subject matter, he displayed an alert interest in our class discussion of the planets.
As usual, he shouted out,

"Teacher…guess what's my favorite planet?"

"I have no idea," I really did.

"My favorite planet is Uranus."

Yup. I knew it.

"That's nice."

"You think Uranus is nice too?"

"Sure."

There were a few giggles from the class. I expected it. These were fifth graders.
I went back to teaching.

"The planets travel in individual orbits and some have moons."

"Uranus has moons? Two, right?"

"I don't know. As I was saying, each planet has unique features…"

He shouted out,

"Teacher, …I'm curious, is Uranus like, really big?"

"Yes, it's huge. It's one of the largest objects in our Solar System."

"I thought so."

"Each planet revolves around the Sun at its own pace and…yes?"

This time he raised his hand.

"Yes Justin?"

"Teacher…is there life, or any living things like little bugs crawling around Uranus?"

Louder laughter

"Unlikely. Living conditions there could not support life as we know it."

I stayed teacher-like, continuing, "The planets revolve around the sun. Each planet…"

He raised his hand again.

"Yes?"

"Er………is Uranus hot?"

"I'm not sure about that."

"You seem very interested in today's subject. Why don't you do some research and look it up?"

I made the mistake of not clearly thinking about my suggestion…

"You want me to look up Uranus?"

"Only if you'd like to."

The class roared with each of his questions. They knew what I knew. It was time to fight back.

"Teacher, I'm wondering. Does Uranus smell?"

"No, not at all Justin. But I'm sure Uranus does!"

LAUREN BACALL'S UNDERWEAR

It was a perfect summer day for lunch in the Hamptons.

As Gina was dressing, I paged through the newspaper to see what was happening on the East End.

A clothesline art exhibit, an estate auction, and a horse show. A notice for a celebrity fundraiser filled part of the page. The money would be raised through public bidding on objects donated by the famous residents of Sag Harbor, Southampton, East Hampton, and the other exclusive villages sharing the sandy peninsula.

TV often featured the wealthy and well-known folks who summered behind the lush hedges of the South Fork. Albee, Stewart, Bacall, Vonnegut, Capote, Pollack, de Kooning, De Nero, Brinkley… regulars all, in the exclusive ocean-front communities.

We picked up Janet and Mario and headed East.

I suggested attending the celebrity fundraiser.

The other three had no interest.

Truth was, neither did I.

"I'm sure Lauren Bacall donated something. Most likely her underwear. I want to bid on her underwear."

"We'll drop you off."

"No really. I want to be the high bidder on her underwear. Let's go."

The laughter eventually ceased, but I didn't.

Finally,

"Will you stop already!"

It wasn't a question. It was an irritated order.

I cut back but didn't stop completely. I'd mumble about how much I really wanted to drive home with the silk treasure in my possession.

When the exasperation started, I wisely went quiet

After eating lunch in the back room of Silver's on Main Street,
Gina and Janet left the restaurant as Mario and I took care of the check.
The women were yards in front of us as Mario slowed to my 4-point gait.
We walked close to the glass storefronts, browsing.
A door was forcefully pushed open by a woman holding two shopping bags.
She walked into — and got tangled by — my left crutch, knocking me off-balance.
I started to fall.
Dropping her bags, she quickly clutched me, held me up until I regained my footing, and righted myself.
She exhaled a puff of air, saying,

"I'm so sorry. Please excuse me. I didn't see you. I wasn't paying attention to where I was going. I hope that you're ok"

"I'm fine. Thanks so much for grabbing me. You prevented me from getting hurt."

It was her. I just couldn't get the words out.

"I drove out here to bid on your underwear."

LEE

We saw the flashing lights as we drove from the beach.

Tommy said, "Pull the car over. Let's check this out."

I stopped behind the squad car making sure not to block the driveway to the Old Field Club.

In this uneventful neighborhood, the constable's car typically was a one-man operation, so it was unusual to see two heads.

The motorcyclists, with their engines still spluttering, sat side by side, some fifty feet in front of the patrol car, its lights throbbing yellow and red.

The driver's door opened. A black boot hit the ground. It had to be Lee.

Lee, the cop who gave me a ticket on that rainy Port Jefferson night a few years back.

My front tires breached the white line by a short step, and he decided that the offense deserved a summons.

He was tucking it under the wiper when we walked out of Grammas with ice cream cones.

We argued in the downpour. I said, "It's so slight, and we're eating ice cream. What could be more innocently American?"

He pointed to the tire and barked, "You crossed the line."

His jacket matched his knee-high black boots. As he gestured, the leather squeaked.

"Why don't you prevent some real crime?"

"Why don't you observe the parking rules?"

My wife said, "Let's just go."

I yanked the dripping ticket from the windshield. Good night," I said as I entered the car. "I'm going home and getting into my dry bed. Enjoy the rest of your shift in a wet woolen uniform."

The scene quickly made sense. Lee was breaking in a trainee and was schooling him in "tough guy."
Maybe the bikers had been speeding or maybe exceeding the local noise ordinance. There was no *maybe* about the tickets they'd each be receiving.

Shoving the car door closed, he hitched up his belt, secured the eight-pointer on his head, and started strutting toward the helmeted bikers.
As he reached the midpoint, the two engines roared and made a soft turn onto the crown of the road and raced away.
Lee pulled out his gun and held it at eye-level with straight-elbowed arms. Each of the two blasts delivered a thick flash of fire. The bikers crossed the belly of the hill and disappeared.
Lee ran to the patrol car and raced off as his tires spit gravel toward us.

We sat there, stunned, pointlessly asking each other, "Did you see that?"
We agreed that Lee was surely schooling a rookie, impressing him with his tricks and techniques.
While we were still absorbing the event, a Suffolk County police car pulled up, followed by Lee's car. They spoke briefly, then the officer approached us.

He asked if we witnessed the event.
We saw it all.

"The constable stated that they attempted to run him over, causing him to employ his weapon. Can you confirm that?"

I suggested that I had no idea what the officer thought, but the shots were fired at two fleeing backs.

That week, *The Herald*, the local paper, always hungry for news, covered the usual smashed mailboxes and arguments between neighbors.
The shooting never was mentioned.

The escaped bikers, with their helmets and roaring engines probably never knew what didn't hit them.

ON HAVING A DOG

 It took me years to grasp the meaning. To fully grasp the undeniable truth.
Yes, dog is man's best friend. Woman's too.
I turn away from the TV solicitations airing abused dogs.
I despise those who did the abusing, as I do the cultures that consider them food.

As I write this, Mugs is undergoing surgery.
He's been out of our home for two days now, but not a bit out of our minds.
We're stressed, and we look it. Dinner didn't taste good last night and I couldn't listen to ugly, angry politics. We're worried.

When a dog nightly sleeps in the bed…
Under the covers…
With his snoring head on the pillow…
His breath touching your neck…
While his absence provides more room, it causes so much more hurt.
How can 33 pounds of solid take over a home and two hearts?

I've had dogs before. And, of course, lost them.
In the end, we always lose them.
That's my only gripe with them…not living longer.
They tutor us in both, loving and grieving.

Sandy always acted brave. He wasn't.
He got too close to that chaine-up monster who tore into his belly.

Tallinn. The bigger the dog, the shorter the life.
Gina cooked and shredded chicken every night, hoping the paleness in her droopy eyelids would get flushed with a healthy red again.
No.

It hurt so badly. Each time.
But each time, I went on.

I was hoping today would be different. I'm still hoping and encouraged by the promising call from the vet.

I did the human numbers along with dog-year math.
If the underwriter's equation holds true, Gina would in time, mourn him alone.
We had our wills redone, assured by our lawyer that we weren't those crazy loons one reads about. The documents specify that he'd be 'adopted' by our housekeeper — our friend — who loves him. As he does her. She talks to him in Portuguese. He howls back.
No one else can do that to him.
He'd be provided for, well beyond his needs and anticipated years.
I joked that he is wealthier at seven than I was at forty.

Yes, I admire the people who save a dog from euthanasia.
They are heroes. Truly loving people.
My neighbors, Chris and Donna, saved a little, pointy nosed, blind Terrier from her likely fate.
They nursed Betty for years. If for nothing else, they'll always have my admiration.

But Mugs is a designer-dog, propagated amuse and be adorable. He does and is.
We bought him eight years ago. A French Bulldog. A Frenchie.
He was the one crawling on top of his litter-mates.
Gina placed him in my arms and I never let go.
She drove home while he sat, wrapped in a blanket, shivering on my lap.
He had a black spot near his nose. In time, I'd dub it the 'Mark of Satan.'
During the first few days in his new home, he cased the joint, before completely taking over.

If he were a child, we'd be called up by the principal. Often.

He has an agenda. But it's not hidden.
It's right out there.
Give me food. Share your food with me. I want affection. Now.
No politics. No religion. No attitudes.

I've lost family members.
It hurt.
But losing him would hurt no less.

The vet called to say that the surgery went well.
We can pick him up tomorrow.

Mugs

SPIT HAPPENS

I learned about it at work where my vantage point was unique.

It had nothing to do with insight or native intelligence.

It was about parking.

All the teachers — the whole staff, — randomly parked their cars facing the building each day.

Not me.

Being handicapped, I parked in the very front. Same spot every day. Thirty-four years of perpendicular consistency.

My uniform perspective was unlike the rest.

For most of the school year it made no difference, but as the warm days approached, it happened.

On an almost daily basis, someone would stop by my car for a brief, after-school chat.

Nice.

Unlike the days of fall, or early spring, the subject, standing beside my open car window, would be backlit by the brilliant sun, providing my eyes with intermittent shade or piercing rays as they varied their position by inches.

During their part of the conversation, I made my discovery.

People spit while speaking. The intensity and position of the sun illuminated the speckled silver fireworks.

And I don't mean some people, or sometimes.

Everybody. Even the refined librarian who always held her crustless sand-wiches with two hands.

I'm no exception.

And I'm not addressing the occasional, renegade spittle.

It's a steady and consistent drizzle.

Furthermore, I learned that words which required a certain configuration of the tongue or lips created splattering cascades.

Especially prefixes which were *par*-ticularly *pre*-dictable.

The more I looked, the less I listened.

I shortened conversations with those who were angry or excited, because they created monsoon-like conditions.

My suspicions had developed years before, while sitting in Row A of The Basic Training of Pavlo Hummel.

I lost interest in the play, but was mesmerized by the collateral moisture from Al Pacino's emotional monologue.

The volume and thrust of the spittle wet the stage as well as my shirt.

Maybe that's why the front part of the stage is called, 'The apron.'

I'm convinced that people dining and conversing together are spitting all over each other's food.

I've been tempted to clutch onto the menu and set it up like a shield on the incoming side of my plate.

When occasional singers would approach our table to take a request, I'd tip, but pass on the song, assuming that it would be a much wetter medium.

But I never seriously considered dining alone.

No. I'd miss the companionship of breaking bread… moist bread.

Anyway, as I once read on a baby's bib.….spit happens.

POST MORTEM

"Don't mention food in there."

I followed the advice upon entering the room with the bright lights and stainless-steel tables. But foolishly, I thought about a food that resembled the overpowering smell.

The body — the partial body — the work of sea scavengers, was face up on the furthest table.
It had lingered deep in the ocean, until the warm summer water allowed gasses to form, giving it buoyancy. Then, carried by the current until a strong wave urged it up to the high-water mark where it was snagged by a branch.
The staff called her a 'wet floater.'
Being my first, I thought of her as Eve.

The forensic pathologist started with the paperwork. Lots of it. Where was the body found? By who? When? Notations were made on the outlined anatomical chart...anterior and posterior. Pathology. Scars. Birthmarks. Tattoos. Piercings.

X-rays and photographs were taken.

He tied a heavy rubber apron over his grey scrubs before putting his hands into the chainmail gloves.
Seeing my puzzlement, he explained,

"If I slip with the scalpel, they'll protect my hands from who knows what."

This doctor was trained in the silent language. Surely, he knew what to look for.
I thought of the words spoken by Dr Hirsch at a lecture years ago:

"The dead talk to the living. They leave clues."

As the clothing was removed for photographs and measurements,
the shifting disturbed a few small crabs who scurried out, clattering across
the steel table.
Labels and sizes were noted. A woolen coat. Blouse. Pants. Panties.
The clothing indicated early winter. She washed up in July.
That helped determine time of death.
Growths…*adipocere*… each with their own maturity cycle, further helped
establish the
timeline.

Eve was a black woman. The x-ray indicated normal bone-mass and slight
arthritis. She was thirty or so.
What remained of her uterus and the etched line across her abdomen sug-
gested children. Perhaps two.
Her height was estimated. Without legs, they were proportioned in.
Maybe five foot six? Of course, no shoes.
Weight extrapolated to one hundred fifty pounds.
No bullet or knife wounds. No mechanical skin penetration.
A faint stain of tobacco suggested right-handed.
No wedding ring.
A nearly full set of well tendered Teeth.

The Y, cut with the rib shears, opened the body like a valise.
Bile, blood, urine, aqueous humor, and spinal fluid, drawn or ladled, and
volumes noted.
Organs removed, examined, weighed, crosscut on the dissection table, with
representative samples recorded, stored, and sent to Toxicology.
The scalp was opened and peeled forward. A round saw hummed across the
skull, creating small puffs of bone dust.
I expected the brain to come out in a contained mass…but was told it decom-
poses quickly. It spilled out into a thick puddle.

A determination is made, maybe. Cause and manner of death. All the parts are returned to the chest cavity which is sewn up and reconstructed for the family's purposes.

I left the building to warm sunlight.
Rather than feeling a weight from the day pushing down on me, I felt light. Happy.
Exhilarated.
I felt very alive.
I drove East, listening to music and smiling at the other drivers.

Dinner was waiting for me.

RIO GRANDE

We passed a sign, *Do not pick up hitchhikers.*
There were none.
I peeked through the wheel and was startled by the ninety.
My senses said we were doing sixty, tops.
The rental was moving, but no reference was visible, no object whizzed past,
no tree, parked car, nothing. Just level horizon.

When a northbound driver finally flashed by, probably misjudging his own
pace, the suction briefly rocked us together.
I thought of that problem — two trains leave their stations and pass at Noon
— and wondered if that other driver considered our fleeting math.

The lone interruption, the only landmark above the flatness, were the elbow-
shaped mounds of Las Cruces.
Our speed didn't appear to be bringing them any closer than they were an
hour ago.
It seemed like we were driving in an Escher rendering where the stairs lead
back to the starting place.

Another sign.

New Mexico State Prison

Hitchhiker? Prison?
I connected those dots.

More flatness, and barely a pulse in the road to rhythmically tighten my
jaw to.
Cruise Controlling a road as straight as a plumb line, I pictured Pacino in
Scent of a Woman. A blind man behind a convertible's wheel.
This would be the place to try it.

The visual estimate was hours off, but we finally approached the stone loaves of Las Cruces, which we skirted on Route 25.

Now behind us, they centered in my rear view, lingering.

Merging with Route 10 meant El Paso was within the hour.

Off to the left was nothing but distance.

To the right was a lesson in Texas cattle.

And more cattle. And more cattle.

And miles of cattle, all trough-bound and facing the road, right to the edge of twilight, where we made the sharp left at the water.

A cramped city of corrugated shacks, lean-tos, and shanties squatted along the bend of the narrow stream.

Our side had taller buildings of brick and stone.

TERANGA

The street was dark. The only glow came from the cloud-filtered moonlight. Falling far behind the other three, their conversation disappeared. They couldn't naturally slow to my four-point gait. Then the jolt came.

One on each side of me. They just appeared. No sound of footsteps. Maybe they weren't wearing shoes. Two men. Young. Maybe in their twenties. Both a deep black. Not the coffee color we call hyphenated-black in America. This was African black.

They spoke softly to each other...almost a whisper. Their words had to be Wolof.

I would have recognized French. The whispers were designed to not alert my three distant companions. The pair continued to walk along at my now quickened, yet still slow pace, almost brushing against my two crutches. I knew I was in trouble.

It had rained moments before we walked down the airplane stairs. The ground was wet and steamy. With the excitement of tourists, the four of us took in what we could from the bus. Taxis, trucks, and cars coughed dark puffs of sulfur exhaust.

Motorbikes gnatted their way along the red dirt shoulder.

Low concrete buildings and tin lean-tos squatted like foothills before dense trees with trunks painted white to eye level.

Women wearing boubous walked along the edge of the road with bundles balanced on their heads. Others, with plastic repurposed soda cases filled with wares.

Some had babies swaddled to their backs.

Primitive wooden carts with car tires pulled by horses strutted by.

A man kneeling on the shoulder of the road was lapping up water from a puddle...dog-like. We were advised that Dakar was the Paris of Africa. No. This was not Paris.

The Teranga was a presentable hotel that modestly lived up to the meaning of its name, Welcome. The façade was tiled in a Mondrian fashion.
It was the base of our daily explorations.

Why were so many of the men along the streets scratching their crotches through their kaftans? Body lice, crabs.
Why were there so many people with glazed, slate colored eyes? Parasites from the water.... river blindness.
Why was a twig hanging from so many mouths? A piece of a special tree used as a toothbrush.

Women were mostly covered from neck to foot by crayon-colored fabrics with
geles wrapped around their heads. Braids and cornrows were worn by young girls.
A mother sat on the sidewalk picking up found grains of white rice which she fed directly to her baby.
The markets were mostly blankets on the ground covered with melons, millet, sorghum, peanuts, and beans. Ebony carvings and straw baskets sat under portable tent roofs.

The rusty ferry spluttered to Gorey Island where we stared through the Door of No Return; the African point nearest to North America providing the shortest ocean journey for the ships laded with enslaved people.
The beach had heavy, brightly colored fishing boats draped with patched nets.

Tooba, the driver who took us North through the desert to Saint Louis, laughed when I answered his question, saying I had only one wife.
The drive took several hours, made even longer by the stops forced by motorcycle police who demanded tribute along the way.
The sand started getting progressively whiter...whiter...brilliant white.
Then the cement plant became visible. After passing it, the white slowly faded back to sand.

Camels walked across our path. Vultures tore flesh from a half]-buried carcass.

The isolated Baobabs, with incredibly broad trunks, held up sparse foliage. We passed grass hut villages.

Saint Louis had an open trench oozing lime colored liquid in the center of the street.

We stopped at a restaurant, asking Tooba to join us. He spit his fish bones onto the dirt floor. Several diners had tribal scarring patterned on their faces... crosshatching, vertical lines, swirls.

I tried to communicate with a young boy, asking if the 'KO' on his tee shirt was his name. He said, "Mohammad Ali.... knock out."

We departed before dark set in.

Tooba stopped at a roadside tree with a man squatting under it. A dead animal, covered with flies, hung head down from a branch. Le boucher used a knife to cut a block of flesh from the carcass. Tooba paid some CFA francs, and tossed the meat into the trunk, explaining that it was for one of his wives. We paid more bribes on the drive home.

As the two continued at my pace, I called out to my companions with the deepest, most assured voice I could.

They heard me, stopped walking, and turned around.

I said, "Wait for me."

I tightened for the lunge.

The shove.

The grab.

They were gon e.

Gone just as they came.

Market in Dakar, Senegal

Tooba, Our Driver

THE BOOKS

Watching Gina cull out her growing cookbook collection, I decided to take an inventory of my own small library. The combined width of the three maroon volumes caught my attention; The History of Long Island, B.F. Thompson's masterwork. They were rare and pricey when I bought them some fifty years ago, well before we moved to Setauket, Thompson's 1784 birthplace.
His wooden home still stands and is open to the public a few days each week.

Before I read the begats and degrees of latitude in Volume One,
my passion for Long Island History had become overshadowed by schoolwork. After squatting unread on my shelf for half a century, maybe it was time I parted with them. I had heard conversations about how easy it was to sell things on eBay. My wife, still busy thinning out her books, didn't have time to guide me.
I guessed it wouldn't be difficult.

After a few mouse clicks, I located the selling tab which directed me to, *Interested in selling books.*
A new window asked for the year of publication.
Third edition, 1962, hardcover.
Then, *Asking price* popped up. I had never given it much thought. After seeing the commission that eBay would earn, I decided to sell the books for $100 apiece. $300 for the set.

Within a few days an email arrived with, *Congratulations.* A buyer had purchased the set with the winning bid of $34.33. The purchaser, Todd Montefusco of Texas, noted that he already sent his check to Pay Pal, which covered the winning bid as well as the commission.
I promptly replied. "This is a mistake. I put the books up for sale, not for bid."

He explained how I entered the information incorrectly.
Although disappointed, he was quite reasonable in accepting my apology.

He said that he owned the older edition, but valued it too much to flip through the pages like a textbook. That was his plan for my books. He explained that his roots were in Setauket. As a child, he lived minutes from the Thompson House.

I assured him that I'd return his payment. I did.

We continued writing to each other.

During his college years he had a summer job at the Stony Brook Museum, taking care of Ward Melville's horse drawn vehicle collection.

I told him that I enjoy writing about events in my life.

He wrote how his little town of Magnolia reminds him of Setauket.

I asked what brought him to Texas.

He explained how he saw the Kennedy assassination on TV.

Soon afterward, he watched as the accused killer, Lee Harvey Oswald was being escorted out of the Dallas jail by Detective James R. Leavelle, who was wearing a tan suit and a Stetson hat. The two men were shackled together. As they slowly maneuvered their way through the crowd of photographers and reporters, a man suddenly entered the frame, brandishing a .38 caliber Colt Cobra revolver. He pulled the trigger, killing Oswald with a single bullet to the abdomen. Leavelle was still chained to the slumping body. Todd explained how the image made a permanent impression upon him. He was inspired to move to Texas 16 years later to pursue a career in law enforcement and to ultimately become a Texas lawman, like Leavelle.

He always wanted to reach out to the man in the Stetson to let him know how much that TV image inspired and influenced him.

Years after being sworn in as a Harris County Deputy Sheriff, he managed to arrange a personal meeting with the iconic detective.

Although Todd and James were separated by 38 years, they quickly became close friends, regularly sharing meals and stories. Over dinner one night, Todd learned that James was a sailor stationed on the U.S.S. Whitney at Pearl Harbor on December 7, 1941. Another landmark date and an even bigger hero.

During his ninety-second birthday dinner, the long-retired Detective presented Todd with the off-duty pistol he carried as a Dallas Police Homicide Detective.

A Colt Model 1908 .380 Hammerless Pocket Automatic Pistol.

I looked at the three volumes frozen on the shelf, thinking that it was time I finally read them. I wrote back to Todd, explaining that I recently added an attachment to my Last Will and Testament.

I bequeath my set of B.F. Thompson's "The History of Long Island" to Todd Montefusco of Magnolia , Texas.

THE HAPPY ENDING

~This is a true story up to the point where it's not~

Susan walked away from her classroom and teaching career.
She would begin a new life.
A fresh start.

But the plan to construct a larger, all-season East Hampton home on the family plot, collapsed under the weight of complex zoning codes.
The well had to find adequate distance from the cesspool and, equally, from the neighbor's property line.
There just wasn't enough land to conform to their demands.
The project became a geometric impossibility.
Susan and John, the architect, drove off separately, never to meet again.

She'd leave the cottage as it was; a small, mostly neglected, summer refuge.
Plants continued to grow from the gutters.... until the accumulating weight brought them down.
Rot advanced across the wooden support beams, giving the little building a noticeable tilt.
She rarely made the drive to visit the place.
Her East End future was past.

This disappointment provided a gift of unplanned opportunities.
She rediscovered... no, actually discovered... the very home she had been living in since childhood.
No longer bound by the calendar and clock of a teacher, she allowed the days to blossom. Her town was a place of surprises; little shops tucked away like unwrapped gifts, the rapture of the winter beach, and neighbors who shared interests and sought to harvest more.

The same hands that learned to develop the reflex movements of knitting wool were soon clutching the oars of the team shell as it glided through the dark water of Huntington Harbor.

The days were rich with discovery.

Ignoring the hard pulse of Mondays, she took slow drives to her cousin's at Point Lookout.

Her strolls on the beach were as varied as the weather.

Susan never before had the proper time for a pet or a worthy cause.

Now she considered both.

Alberto...Alberrrrto...was a puppy with a promise.

The Guide Dog Foundation would allow Susan one year to nurse him through his training and schooling, until he could guide a blind person away from the perils of daily life.

Susan quickly fell into deep love with this magnificent pup.

Although not able to roll the 'r' in his name, she let him roll into her heart.

His thick, rust-colored hair contoured his trunk in tight ringlets.

The arctic-white teeth felt like affectionate pins when he'd nuzzle her fingers.

When carsickness was no longer the big question, there was no question about his future.

Susan was never far from Alberto.

Libraries, theatres, and restaurants welcomed him and his yellow vest. When Susan looked at the menu, a glass would be put on the table and a dish would be placed on the floor.

He was not a mere pet.

He was a working man.

While slow at first, he got his footing and developed into a craftsman, know-ing that play and business were very different events.

He stopped at curbs and avoided obstacles.

He learned to ignore dogs while he was working.

Alberto became a master.

The day came when Alberto was ready to offer his services to a sightless person. It would be a wonderful day. It would also be a sad day.

Susan would lose her friend. Her dearest buddy.

She opened the car door and Alberto eagerly sprung to the ground. He'd guide her one last time through the Foundation's red door.

The papers were signed.

The equipment, the harness, the apron, were returned.

All that was left was the deep hug, and then, the slow, lonely walk to the car without Alberto.

Susan sat in the car …staring at the steep roof of the building. She pushed the tears to the back of her eyes. Her home would feel so empty.

~Here's the part I made up~

Susan turned the key to begin the lonely drive home, but the car offered no response. After trying again, she stepped out to lift the hood.

Knowing nothing about the internal combustion engine, she thought that the upturned hood would be an appeal for help from a kindly motorist.

She gave the soundless engine a perfunctory look.

A loose battery cable, twisted up like a cowlick, drew her attention. It was that simple. An unattached cable.

While attempting to push it back into its proper setting, it stroked against the other cable, made a brief snapping sound before causing an explosion. The battery violently split into pieces… acid sprayed out in every direction, including into Susan's face. She screamed.

A painful sting. A cold, blistering sensation on her skin.

Although her eyes were fully open, she saw nothing.

She repeatedly blinked to wash out the searing burn.

But nothing.

She yelled, "I'm blind! I'm blind!"

After taking a few cautious steps, leaning her hip against the security of the car, she felt the springy coldness of the chain link. She inched her way along as she clutched handfuls of fence that led her toward the red door. She found the handle.

She yelled, "Alberto…Alberto…I'm blind!"

Susan

THE INCIDENT

It was happening again. Much like that rainy night years ago.
I didn't know why I signed out 'that' book from all the thousands in the library. The spasms were brusque electric jolts between my calf and ankle. Restless, and failing to sleep, I tilted the bed light toward the italicized date. July 29th, 1890.
One hundred years to the day, the great Dutch artist pressed the pistol to his head.

I thought back to that sleepless evening because it was happening again. The spasms came in irritating intervals, providing just enough pause to lure me — teasing me — into a soft sleep before striking again.

The abrupt light from the iPad made me squint.
No emails at this deep hour, other than ads sent by robots.
Facebook was sleeping. Even California Facebook. I thought back to the family incident. I was young. Five? Six? I remember pajamas and early morning. The adults were talking seriously. No laughter.
Uncle Gene stood by the door. He never moved beyond that spot. His thick hair had some strands breaking straight up. I liked the way it always had those unplanned, renegade spikes. He was wearing a brown leather jacket with an emblem —a patch — on the chest. It might have been about the Air force. He'd been in the service before becoming a cop.

Something was wrong.

"They put a casket in front."
In front of what? I thought.

"There was a screwdriver."
What about a screwdriver?

He didn't stay long. I mostly stopped thinking about it, and rarely asked. Except for that day when my mother quietly explained.

"He shot a man. A black man who held a screwdriver.
The man died. People protested and put a casket in front of the police station."

No one else ever said a word about it. I understood not to ask again, even during those rare family visits. He'd have my father hide his gun and bullets in separate places, away from the curiosity and reach of us kids, then he'd talk and tell jokes.
Some were about black people, but he used a different word.

When Uncle Gene retired, his son prepared to join the force. And, like his father, he too used the different word.

I threatened to warn the authorities. He'd never get hired.
I didn't, but they both stopped talking to me for years.
Uncle Gene died from emphysema.

My cousin became a cop in the same precinct wearing his father's badge.

Years later, after meeting by chance, we reunited by phone, talking about baseball, Atlantic City, and Jersey drivers. Safe stuff.
During one conversation, I nervously asked him if he would mind telling me about the incident. He answered with words that explained nothing. I never asked again.

He got ill. He started gasping through our conversations. He too, died from emphysema.
It was over.

Another jolt kept me from sleeping. I started tapping into Google.
Searching.

Black man killed by cop in Bronx New York.

Black man killed by cop. Bronx New York / Gene Stasiuk

Black man killed by cop. Bronx New York / Eugene Stasiuk

And then…it appeared on the screen.

Unsolved Civil Rights Murder Cases…1934-1970.

There were hundreds of names.

Page 182…Part 2: The Forgotten
Charles Phifer….January 16, 1949: The Bronx, NY

Patrolman Eugene Stasiuk answered a call to the home of Mrs. Anne Phifer,
who was engaged in a quarrel with her stepson.
Stasiuk shot and killed Charles Phifer, claiming self-defense, although Phifer was
shot in the back and unarmed.
Investigators deemed the slaying "justified."

THE LITTLE BOY WHO SAVED THE WORLD

Billy was the baby.

Besides being the youngest, his freckles, red hair, and cowlick, quite naturally attracted the affections of his parents and two older siblings , Elaine and Eddie.

The family fussed over him. He felt special and secure.

It didn't last long.

When Jean was born, Billy lost many benefits of being the youngest.

More were lost after Ann was born. Then Helen. Then Richie.

By the time Beth came — to permanently be crowned "baby of the family" — he was just another kid.

It was fortunate that Billy's father was a Doctor...Doctor Bodkin...a urologist, because his income had to feed ten mouths. Eleven, counting Ginger, the Golden Retriever.

His mother, Miriam, had so much work to do at home — the laundry, the cooking, the cleaning — there was no time for her to add an income.

When Billy went off to school, he learned Math, History, and Reading, along with Duck and Cover. Duck and Cover would protect Billy from a thing Miss Berry called, "The escalating arms race."

Ron Klemici asked the teacher, "What's so dangerous about arms?"

'No, Ron, not arms like arms and legs. Arms like armies and armaments. Weapons. Bombs."

She explained that two countries possessed incredible devices...Atomic bombs. America had thousands of them. But so did the other powerful country. Our enemy. Russia.

The teacher said that if we ever had war with them, or, if they ever decided to attack us first, the blast, the heat, and the radioactive fallout would surely kill us all.

The class watched the film, Bert the Turtle. If a bombing was suspected, Bert would drop to the ground (Duck) and retreat into his shell (Cover).

So Billy, along with his classmates, was instructed to practice dropping to the floor and retreating under their wooden desks. But he wasn't convinced that desks would protect them from an atomic bomb…the blast, the heat, the radioactive fallout.
Because he was smart, he was also scared.

His scoutmaster mentioned that the supreme leader of Russia, Nikita Khrushchev, would be traveling to New York. The very man who threatened America by saying, "We shall bury you."
Billy thought that those Russians must be monsters.

He asked his mother what such horrible people looked like. She pointed out that Helen, their neighbor, while not exactly Russian, was Ukrainian…a close match. Billy didn't think that
she looked evil. Maybe there was hope.

If he could just somehow communicate with Nikita Khrushchev, maybe he could convince him to never use those atomic weapons. Billy shared his fear with no one except his mother.
He also told her about the letter he wrote in his bedroom at night, using his best pencil penmanship.

It was a touching appeal. Billy simply wanted to live. Live in peace. He was sure that young children in Russia felt as he did. They too, probably wanted to play, to grow up, to learn, to have a safe future. He attached his school photo. How would he get it to the man with the bombs?

His mother knew. She helped him address the envelope in ink.

Chairman Nikita Khrushchev,
c/o Soviet Delegate to the U.N.
New York, NY.

He licked and applied the three-cent stamp.
For months Billy thought about the letter. Maybe it was foolish.
Maybe he made a mistake by bringing attention to himself.
Perhaps some Russian agents would hunt him down...an easy mission with his return address, and photo.

Billy grew up. Joined the Marines. Went to college. Became a teacher. Husband. Father.

He attended a seminar on the Cold War. The guest speaker was the Professor of International Studies at Princeton University, Dr. Sergei Khrushchev, the son of Nikita.
After the compelling lecture, Billy approached Dr. Khrushchev.

He started by saying, "When I was a young boy, I sent a letter to your father about my fear of a nuclear war."

Billy knew what would happen next.
Dr. Khrushchev would put his hands on Billy's shoulders.
Silently, he would stand there...staring.
Finally, he would speak....

"Were you that little boy?"

Billy would answer,

"Why, yes I was."

Dr. Khrushchev would then say,

'My father carried your letter in his pocket, every day, every day...right up to his death. There was a time during the missile crises when our Russian generals gathered in the War Room to prepare a preemptive nuclear strike against America.

Father took out your letter and read it to the military leaders.

The generals listened intently. They sat back quietly, then voted to cancel the attack."

Dr Khrushchev would have a tear in his eye.

So would Billy.

**The little boy...with the cowlick... who saved the world
is in the back row, standing next to the teacher.**

GEORGE

Everybody got to know him. He wouldn't allow anyone not to.
A slight guy with red hair and protruding ears, flitting from lounge to lounge,
chatting as he made his way around the main pool.
One 'lap' could take hours.
Our winter getaways meant warm weather, friendly Mexicans, and George.

He was a used-car salesman from Saint Louis. His confident voice had
a crispness,
especially when sharing his adventures. Some seemed fabulous…hard to
believe. But each was confirmed with a resigned, *"Yes, it's true,"* from Lynn.
She was his wife. Pretty, younger, quiet, and a church lector who was content
to read under a clump of palm trees, working on her book reviews for the
Post Dispatch. She was friendly, but clearly not eager to fill her vacation with
resort babble. She'd politely pause to authenticate George's tales when asked.

"Was he really in a movie with Lana Turner?"

"Yes. *Love Has Many Faces.* It was shot here, on the beach."

"Did he actually hang out with the cast…Cliff Robertson, Carlos Montalbán,
Stefanie Powers, and Hugh O'Brian?"

"He did. And some time after making the film, he ran into O'Brian in Cannes,
who treated George to lunch, along with Princess Soroya, the Shah's wife."

"He actually entered Havana from the mountains in Castro's jeep entourage?"

"Yes, he was there during the revolution, but he doesn't talk much about how
he fled the country."

His stories were true.
I stopped asking for verification.

One was the Vegas Caper.

George hung with the second string, bench players, of the notorious Rat Pack.

Corbett Monica, Joey Bishop and a few lesser-lesser- knowns.

Some of the crew crossed the border to Tijuana for a fun weekend.

Lenny was tempted by a prostitute and, as he was fully engaged, had his clothes stolen and discarded by George.

Lenny was left naked in Tijuana, laughing but seeking revenge.

He and the others plotted.

Meeting in a Vegas bar, they served George a Tom Collins. Being a non-drinker, he resisted. They talked him into it, saying, "C'mon George, let's toast to a lifetime friendship."

He remembered picking the drink up, but not putting it — almost carried — him onto the plane. They departed with his wallet, money, and ID, leaving George sleeping with a one-way ticket to Honolulu half-tucked into his shirt pocket.

He was out through most of the long flight, finally waking to turbulence.

His head was resting on the shoulder of a woman in the aisle seat.

"I'm so sorry. Where am I? Who are you?"

She was a friendly woman

"Why, in about an hour we'll be in Honolulu." Surprised he didn't know.

They chatted.

"What brings you to Honolulu?"

"I'm on a business trip."

"What type of business? Insurance? Investments?"

"Whipped cream."

"Are you kidding?"

"No, I inherited my family's business… Reddi-Wip."

At the end of her story, she asked about him.

"Looks like I've been sent on a monkey business trip. Well,I have these friends..."

She loved his story.

Upon entering the terminal, he saw the sign.

"Aloha, to Hawaii's Honolulu international airport"
Governor John Anthony Burns

Could it be?

Governor Burns, received his education in St. Louis, and was a member of the exclusive Missouri Athletic Club.

George used to park cars there for the prominent gentlemen of the city, always doing so in a courteous and efficient way.

They members liked him. Popular and affable, he did well with tips.

They called him 'Red.'

George borrowed a quarter to make the call.

The Governor took it and was thrilled to hear from Red.

Yes, of course. He remembered. The ears. The hair. The fine service.

"Red, you just stay right there at the airport. I'll have my driver pick you up."

He was feted like a celebrity at the State Mansion. The toast of dinner guests, he earned his keep by sharing the story with the executive staff, the neighbors, and guests.

The Governor convinced George to stay the week.

When he was ready for the flight home, the Governor insisted on reversing the prank.

He had George fitted with a tuxedo, an orchard lei, and a bouquet of roses.

He ordered the flight crew to roll out a red carpet upon George's arrival in Vegas,

where he had scheduled his friends to pick him up and laugh at the results of his predicament.

The plane emptied.

The attendants unrolled the carpet for the final departing passenger, George... with his tuxedo, lei, and flowers.

The friends didn't laugh.

They stared.

He approached them.

"You won't believe this. The airline informed me that I was their one millionth passenger. They set me up in a hotel. Gave me a car and driver, cash, great dinners. Incredible. Thanks so much guys."

THE CALL

When his daughter called, I knew.
We met in the mid 50's
My family left the South Bronx for Ronkonkoma.
His family spent the summers at their cottage on Kingdom Court.
In front of Joe's house, at the end of my unpaved, dead end street,
Alphy, and his younger brother, Johnny, became my friends.

In the fall, the Sciontis would head back to their real house, somewhere near
the Kosciuszko Bridge.
We didn't see each other during the school year, but we spent our summers
together at the Lake, swimming, trying to win prizes at Turner's Amusement
Park, playing miniature golf at Freddy's, or just looking for adventures...
which we always managed to find.

It went on that way for a few years, until Larry's yellow Pontiac convertible
overturned going around that sharp corner by the train station.
Johnny didn't make it to the hospital.
I knew how Larry drove.
The Sciontis left Kingdom Court, and never returned.

I saw Alphy less, but we never disconnected.
When he got married, I was his best man.
When I got married, he was mine.
Like his father, he became a cop.
I became a teacher.
Christmas Eve meant crab sauce and pasta at Alphy's.
We'd play with his three daughters.
It was on his black and white TV we waited to see Neil Armstrong step onto
the moon.
There was a big distance between our views of the world...but there was none
between our friendship.

He divorced a few years later.

After going through three more failed marriages he changed his email address to 'finally alone'...even though he was living with his mother.

When she died, he sold the house and moved to Stony Brook to live with Jessica's family, a few miles from us.

Missing the solitary life, he eventually bought his own place...a condo in a development restricted to those over fifty five.

He loved it. Always buying a painting, a statue, or a piece of furniture.

He bought a crossbow and sword, preparation for the Muslim apocalypse he was certain was coming.

Not settling for bachelor food, he usually cooked full meals.

We did a lot of talking on FaceTime...marveling at the technology.

With all his intestinal issues he didn't go out much, But whenever he stopped by, he'd bring a gift for us...olive oil, some spice, or a toy for Mugs.

After writing a piece, I'd email it to him.

His reviews ranged from 'great' to 'garbage'.

But they were always honest.

He came by on Tuesday, while I was resting in bed.

Sitting on the bay-window shelf, he tossed a package to me.

A gift.

A book.

Beautiful antique red leather with a string place marker.

I opened it to empty pages. I gave a puzzled look.

"You like to write. Fill it."

"Thanks Alphy. It's beautiful."

After petting Mugs, he was gone.

That evening he prepared dinner, firing up two burners.

He decided to rest in bed as it was cooking.

He fell asleep.

A fire started.

It travelled up, serpent-like, around the cabinets.

His condo filled up with angry black smoke which curled its way across the ceiling before flooding the room.

It seeped into his lungs.

The first breath didn't wake him.

It pushed him into a deeper stillness.

He slept through the fire, as the smoke filled him.

He kept breathing until he stopped.

Someone noticed that the building was on fire.

Two burners were found, still lit.

The medics started his heart.

It stopped.

They tried again.

The hospital could not detect any brain activity.

We were waiting for the heavy snow to stop for the drive to the hospital.

Then Jessica called.

The book Alphy gave me.

THE TOWN HOUSE

 The four of us headed for the city.

I was driving, and Tommy, sitting next to me, was paging through New York Magazine. It was the June, 1980 edition. They ran a cover story on the Nixons and their town house.

He read out loud.

Disgraced and undone by the cover-up of the Watergate burglary and money-laundering scandal, Richard Nixon, after announcing his resignation, moved to La Casa Pacifica, San Clemente, California, where he and Pat lived for five years before settling in Manhattan.

They quickly found a perfect place where they committed a deposit, but the co-op board backtracked when shareholders revolted, objecting that the Nixons would bring notoriety and Secret Service disruptions to the exclusive building. Not wanting an issue, the Nixons agreed to cancel the deal, and continued searching. A couple, the Tanners, wishing to downsize, put their town house up for sale; a 5,000-square-foot, 12-room home at 142 East 65th Street. The four-story, 1871 building on a tree-lined block between Lexington and Third Avenues came with an impeccable pedigree. For about 60 years until his death in 1961, it had been the home of Judge Learned Hand. Next door was David Rockefeller, and over the garden wall on East 64th Street lived Arthur M. Schlesinger Jr., the historian and assistant to John Kennedy; the very man who defeated Nixon in the 1960 presidential election.

They agreed to the $690,000 price, but ran into trouble selling Casa Pacifica and needed those funds to buy the town house. He asked if the closing could be delayed.

"Absolutely not," Mr. Tanner said, amazed that after all the Watergate money changing hands Mr. Nixon was strapped for cash.

They ended up getting a loan from the Key Biscayne Bank owned by their friend, Bebe Rebozo. They purchased the town house."

We came out of the Midtown tunnel to sunshine and headed North.

Gina and Valarie wanted to shop.

Tommy and I didn't.

I looked at the cover of the magazine and came up with the idea, since Nixon's home was a few short blocks from Bloomingdale's.

"You two shop. We'll find something to do. We can all meet at a set time here."

I pointed to the town house photo —142 East 65th.

We dropped the women off near the store.

It was a surprise to find an open parking space right in front of the four story home. The brick section blended with the ivory-colored stone which surrounded long, narrow windows. The roof line was decorated with a heavy cornice. A thin black metal fence seemed designed for appearance rather than security.

There was a buzz…men in suits and earpieces were walking in and out of the large front door. Maybe a dozen. Maybe just a few. They were difficult to count, moving like bees around a hive, and they all looked the same.

One agent stood by us. I started asking questions.

"Are the Nixon's home?"

"They are right now."

"Is there always so much activity here?"

"No. Today's a special day."

"Why special?"

"Today is their 40th wedding anniversary. They're going on a trip."

"Do people make remarks or ask him about Watergate?"

"Actually, no. People tend to be very polite with him."

I looked at the windows across the narrow street. "How do you protect him, for instance, someone shooting him from one of those windows?"

"We can only protect him so much."

The black enamel door opened. Richard Nixon, in a grey suit, and looking very much like the man I had seen on TV hundreds of times, walked over to us. He was short. We shook hands. He asked where we were from.

"Long Island."

"Oh, I have fond memories of the Island."

"I saw you there once. By the airport".

"Yes. I remember. Well, no, I don't remember you. I remember the airport."

We all laughed
We talked about the Mets.

"What a team!"

"Are you enjoying the city?"

"New York is a great city. Much to see and do. Great city."

I thought about the reported comment he made while visiting the Great Wall of China.

My…that is a great wall.

A passerby stopped.

He tried to get into the conversation by saying,

"Mr Nixon, turn to your left."

I put my arm around the former President and responded,

"President Nixon never turns to his left."

Nixon laughed.

"I see that you're using crutches. What, a ski accident?"

Before I could answer, the door opened and Pat came out.

We watched as she walked slowly without saying a word or making eye contact.

I knew she had suffered a stroke.

She was escorted into one of the two light grey vans which were parked right behind us.

President Nixon said goodbye.

"Happy anniversary President Nixon."

"Thank you fellers."

The vans, loaded with the Nixons and the agents, started driving way.
Pat, sitting by the window, put her head against the glass, and looked at me
standing there on my crutches.
With a forlorn face, she moved her head from side to side, mouthing "Sorry."

THE TRAIN TO LÍMON

The tour book foolishly boasted that Limón had rain almost every day and it was the world's only city with vultures walking the streets in search of carrion.

A Tica advised us to take the proper seats. If not, we'd be moving backwards, looking at what passed rather than what was approaching.

The Atlantic Terminal in San Jose was already clattering with both, hawkers and travelers, although the daily departure was over an hour away. A poster above a shrine to the Virgin warned in Spanish that pickpockets and purse snatchers were surely lurking about.

We placed 200 Colones on the counter. The agent, framed by a wrought iron window, pushed two long paper strips toward us. The tickets listed 56 stops along the eight-hour journey.

Paraiso, La Gloria, Monte Verde, Boston, Liverpool, and at the bottom, our destination, Limón.

We chose second-class, though warned that the accommodations were spare. Unpadded boards, peeling paint, and a toilet braced over a hole exposed to the tracks. We wanted to be with the real people.

The seats were pairs of wooden benches facing one another. Each fit two. Maybe three if a small child was in tow. Windows were left open, unless a flash rain would have them drawn down.

The car filled up with mostly black faces, not the light-skinned people of the Central Valley. The Tico Times explained that after San Jose was established, the Jamaican construction workers were cast out of the city and reemployed to clear a jungle path and lay a rail line to the Atlantic coast.

Limón was the seaport destination, created by coffee barons to more easily market their England–bound crop. Before the train, beans grown on the highland plantations were toted in sacks carried by oxcart to the Pacific shore for the long journey around South America. The train eliminated that. The barons planted banana trees along the route, providing food for the laborers.

Those who survived Malaria, dysentery, and heat stroke, developed and settled in villages along the 100 miles of narrow gauge snaking its way to the ort.

A bell clanged. A horn squawked.

The growl of the engine was followed by a reverse lurch. It seemed we picked the wrong bench which would mean eight hours of backward. But the century-old train heaved, then stopped the retreat, slowly grinding its way forward. It churned out of the valley, skirting the surrounding mountains, entering tunnels, and crossing open savannah.

We passed plantations of coffee flowers, banana groves, and cocoa farms, before rattling over a truss bridge which spanned the turbulent river.

A young boy pointed out the open window yelling,

"Mama…la loona, la loona."

An egret was high stepping about the shoreline.

The trees became more frequent along with shadows as we entered the jungle slopes.

The canopy sliced ribbons of early sun that lit the dense growth of tangles, branches, moss, and vines.

A flicker of railroad ties came through uneven cracks parting the wooden floor planks.

The straining engine relaxed, slowing to our first stop. A few travelers boarded, others got off, as hawkers raced to the open windows, waving bananas, breadfruit, papyrus and ice bags to entice the passengers.

Quickly, the engine was throttling to pull us to the next station.

Both sides of the rail line had crude shacks with porches facing, and close to the train. The daily passing was their entertainment artery. With no exception, each little home displayed a yellow or green flag from a pole or tree. A fellow rider advised us that 1986 was a national election year and the big vote was days away.

Again, a stop, more passengers, some departures, peddlers, and off.

Again, and again.

After crossing the Talamanca peaks, we felt the abrupt tilt of the downward journey where the plants changed to hibiscus and shoulder-high wild impatiens. The crackle of birds grew louder and different.

A mother sat on the floor, fired up a crude portable stove, and cooked eggs for her two children.

People waved to us from their porches. More flags.

More starts and stops.

As the sun faded, we could see the primitive shelters glowing from the glowing lantern-light.

Another passenger, an old Tico, with blue-black skin and a Jamaican accent, asked where we were headed.

"Limón."

He waved his index finger, slowly, back and forth...speaking in a solemn voice...

"Do not go to Limón...danger is there."

More stops...transactions....departures... boardings...waves...flags.

The sky was darkening and the rails flattened upon reaching the mangroves of the muggy coastal swamps.

One final stop.

The train hissed and the wheels grated to a halt.

Knowledgeable passengers raced off.

We stepped down to the bare soil.

Two buzzards were pulling at something long dead.

It started to rain.

THE TRIP

Richard Nixon was the president.
Thousands flocked to Woodstock.
Men stepped on the Moon.
The Mets won the World Series,
I was a college student.

The four flights were always an effort.
Handrail, crutch, step, up…
Handrail, crutch, step, up…
My twice weekly effort to beat the crush mobbing the stairway, made me the
first one in the classroom.
Boredom set in quickly, so I reached for a magazine left on a nearby desk.
The International Journal
It was of little interest, so I headed to the back-page ads.

Join the Citizen's Exchange Corps
Travel to the Soviet Union
Help end the Cold War.

It was 1969 and a tense standoff between the superpowers, the U.S. and
the U.S.S.R., both with vast nuclear arsenals, had already produced a sense
of dread.
The Berlin wall was up and the Soviet Union broke the nuclear-test morato-
rium by detonating a hydrogen bomb…the largest explosion ever recorded…
still.
It was the era of fallout shelters, civil defense drills and nuclear war sur-
vival kits.
The dread became an active terror after the Cuban Missile Crisis.

We had been married for a short time and never took a real honeymoon, just
that weekend in Sloansville.

Gina often talked about her fascination with Russian History, and neither of us had ever been on a plane.

I tore out the ad.

After getting home I made the call, thinking that I'd quickly discover that the whole thing couldn't happen.

There would surely be obstacles, and the effort would go down as a thoughtful gesture.

The receptionist answered my questions, took down our details.

I mostly stopped thinking about it.

Gina said Mr. Decker would unlikely give her time off from the new job she started only the month before.

We got a call back a few days later.

It was Stephen Daniel James... the director.

Dan was a one-time advertising copywriter whose unlikely proposal for a Soviet-American citizen exchange program propelled him onto the Cold War stage and led to cultural peace tours in the 1960's.

His plan was to enable citizens of the United States and the Soviet Union to accomplish what their governments would not do... open doors, share ideas, and build mutual trust. He felt that citizen diplomacy was urgent.

He arranged an interview with us.

The talk went well.

He explained that his program had won the support of the White House, the State Department and both Houses of Congress.

Although, Eleanor Roosevelt called his idea rather impractical.

He conferred with Soviet and American diplomats and attended an international peace conference in Africa, attracting enough financial backing to quit his job and work full time advancing his idea.

An expected hurdle developed.

The price for this month-long excursion was beyond our means, so the journey appeared to be over before it began.

Days later we received another call from Dan. He urged me, a quadriplegic, and Gina, a young woman so interested in Russian History, to represent the group in Moscow.

He offered us some rare scholarship money.

Gina's new boss agreed to give her the month off.

Like nesting dolls, the hurdles were getting smaller.

We were given books to acquaint us with Soviet life and customs before we attended the preparatory conference.

It was presented by the women from Glassboro, N.J., the location of a summit meeting in 1967 between President Lyndon B. Johnson and Premier Alexei Kosygin.

The Glassboro group recently returned from an exchange trip and had a lot to share.

We had to dig up birth certificates for passports, get photos, smallpox shots, proof of assorted vaccinations, and visa applications. We had to buy our first ever luggage, take out a loan, get electric adapters, a bathtub plug, buy insurance, get an international driver's license, and make many dozens of phone calls. We were advised, wisely, to pack toilet paper.

Our next meeting was at C.W. Post College to meet our fellow Corps members.

Some twenty people, mostly older than us.

Svetlana was to be our interpreter.

The passports arrived.

The visas were issued.

The barriers were gone.

After one more meeting, a lecture on the rehabilitation of Stalin, we were boarding the Aeroflot plane.

Gina chatting with an African communist.

Lenin…everywhere.

Gina by the Neva River, across from the Kremlin.

Moscow vendor.

Meeting with members of the Communist Party.

CONNECTING THE DOTS

We live on a timeline where each of us gets two dots.

Two terminal dots.

Upon getting the first, authorities issue a certificate.

A warranty.

A limited warranty.

That first dot celebrates a bundle of joy.

The date, noted, and maybe an inked footprint, or a snip of hair for the scrapbook.

Then, off and on our way.

We accumulate more dots.

First tooth.

The religious rituals.

The part in the play.

The game-saving catch.

Graduation.

All the graduations.

That first paycheck.

Marriage, maybe.

Kids, maybe.

Dot, dot, dot.

Some, with more eventful lives, gather trophy dots which dangle like jewels.

That speech.

Award.

Lofty position.

The contract specified two terminal dots per customer.

The other one is out there, but, like gravity, we don't think much about it until we feel its force.

We study the not-so-fine print which plotted the journey from here to there, trying to make it the longest distance between two points.

So, how to use the remainder of our timeline?

We have between now and then to decide before the clock runs out.

Post Mortem:

An old guy…or maybe was he a young guy…once advised me that life is not a dress rehearsal.

It's the real thing.

No do-overs.

No Mulligans.

My mother was there when I took my first breath.

Maddeningly obvious, but important, because

I was there when she took her last.

A symmetry that helps in some way.

After the reception desk, at the end of the long

hall, a turn, last room on the right.

I avoided knowing the town and tried to avoid knowing the date.

The less I knew the less I'd be haunted by geography,

anniversaries, and painful bookmarks.

All pointless burdens.

But no, I overheard, "Hey, it's the first day of spring."

So that's there.

Always there.

Every Year

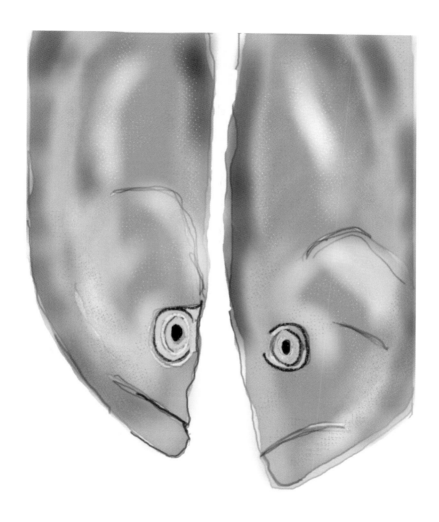